# Central Glass Works

## The Depression Era

Tim Schmidt

Schiffer Publishing Ltd
4880 Lower Valley Road, Atglen, PA 19310 USA

Library of Congress Cataloging-in-Publication Data

Schmidt, Tim.
Central Glass Works : the Depression era / by Tim Schmidt.
p. cm.
ISBN 0-7643-2016-5 (pbk.)
1. Central Glass Co. (Wheeling, W. Va.)--History.
2. Glassware--West Virginia--Wheeling--History--20th century.
I. Title.
NK5205. C45 S35 2004
748.2'09754'14--dc22
2003027128



Designed by Ellen J. (Sue) Taltoan
Type set in Americana XBd BT/Souvenir Lt BT
ISBN: 0-7643-2016-5
Printed in China
1 2 3 4

Published by Schiffer Publishing Ltd.
4880 Lower Valley Road
Atglen, PA 19310
Phone: (610) 593-1777; Fax: (610) 593-2002
E-mail: Info@schifferbooks.com



In Europe, Schiffer books are distributed by
Bushwood Books
6 Marksbury Ave.
Kew Gardens
Surrey TW9 4JF England
Phone: 44 (0) 20 8392-8585; Fax: 44 (0) 20 8392-9876
E-mail: info@bushwoodbooks.co.uk
Free postage in the U.K., Europe; air mail at cost.

# Contents

# Epitaph & Dedication of This Reference

Of all the research material found in trade journals, newspapers, glass house directories, catalogs, flyers, books and any possible place giving a reference to, or on, Central Glass Works, this is by far the most devastating piece of information found. An epitaph that reads like and resembles more a garage sale ad, is all that one of the greatest glass houses in American glass making history is able to achieve after such an illustrious career. This reference is dedicated to the workers of the Central Glass Plant in Wheeling West Virginia.

BANKRUPT SALE
Trustee Now Conducting Sale of All Assets of
Central Glass Works
Wheeling, W. Va.
Manufacturer for 78 years of famous lines of hand-blown ware. Plant operated until just before filing of voluntary bankruptcy proceedings.
FINISHED WARE REAL ESTATE
MOULDS MACHINERY EQUIPMENT
Trustee is authorized to sell all assets (except fixtures) at private sale. Single items or plant as a whole may be purchased. Trustee reserves the right to reject any bid. Plant open for inspection Tuesdays and Thursdays at 10 A. M. to 12 M.
DAILY SALE OF GLASSWARE IN SMALL LOTS AT FACTORY OFFICE, SIXTEENTH AND McCOLLOCH STREETS.
J. WALTER WILLIAMS, Trustee,
1116 McCulloch Street, Wheeling, W. Va.

Central Glass Works Obituary, *Nation Glass Budget,* January 20, 1940.

# Acknowledgments

These are the folks that helped make this reference possible, by lending glass, contributing glass, keeping prices low enough for me to acquire, or just being patient with me during this project. My wife Linda, who for over twenty-six years has been my cornerstone of support and my primary editor. Then there are the kids, Brad and Heather, who while growing up never wanted to see another antique mall or resale shop. Even vacations were scary for them, as I would plan our trips by what antique malls were in the path of our destination. My Dad and Mom, Otto & Jacquelyn Schmidt. And, my adopted mom and dad, Ted & Constance del Solar; for without their love, guidance, patience, and understanding, you would be reading none of this. Jan Reichling and Melissa Bratkovich, for all their help and support! Larry Baker, Michael Krumme, Roni Sionakides, the late Keith Dunn, Neil and Eddie (where's the book?) Unger. Helen Jones, Robert Carlson, the late Jerry Gallagher, John Madeley, Charles Griggs, Liz Engle, the late Pam Ochs, The West Virginia Museum Of American Glass, and the whole crew including the late French Batton. The William Koloseike Family, and the Folks at Schiffer Publishing. Special thanks go out to Dean Six, for also putting up with my madness for over ten years, and recommending this project to the publisher.

# Foreword

Over a decade ago I learned someone in far off Chicago was interested in a then little known glass company in my home state of West Virginia called Central Glass. What followed was a long and often rich exchange of information between this seeker and me. Within that same time the little known company became better known and a few of its patterns began to appear in popular price guides. A book on the early years of the firm was published. Collectors appeared. Interest grew.

Through this all Tim Schmidt continued to ask good, often difficult, questions about this company he was passionately interested in. He traveled far to share his hard won knowledge with collectors and historians. He collected, watched, and learned. Within the massive scope of the nearly 450 hot glass producers having existed in West Virginia over nearly 200 years, Central's history and production is given the attention it deserves in this well documented reference work. I've waited a long time for this book. We will all profit from this work and enjoy the answers to many of those long unanswered attribution questions it provides.

Dean Six<br>
Author & co-founder of the<br>
West Virginia Museum of American Glass, Ltd.

# The Main Objective

The main objective of this book is to provide a reference to glassware made by the Central Glass Works in Wheeling, West Virginia, starting around the early teen years of the twentieth century, through the Great Depression, and up to their closing in 1939. You will find there are some older or pre-depression era pieces shown; this is to remove any confusion regarding whether or not Central made the items—in the past other companies have gotten credit for these wares. Another reason for showing an older item is to increase awareness if it has been reproduced. And, some of the older glass is just too cool not to have it in the book. Since my field of knowledge is mainly glass and dinnerware lines from the depression era, most of what you will see is from that period.

Catalogs for this company are very scarce and highly prized by those who own them. Needless to say, most of the research material has come from trade journals, and some material has come from others who have helped with this project.

If you are not familiar with what depression glass is, the basic depression era glass was mass-produced machine-made glassware that was manufactured during the worst economic times in the United States. Because it was made fast and inexpensively, colors were added to hide imperfections in the pieces. These pieces of glass were handed out at movie theaters, sold at discount stores, or given away as premiums for trading with merchants. Plates and other items were given away in sacks of flour or oats and people started collecting beautiful colored dinnerware free in this fashion. Other ways pieces were acquired would be to spend a pre-determined amount of money with a grocery store or other retail merchant and receive a punch card, much like grocery stores still do today. After a determined amount was spent, the buyer would receive possibly a complete dinner setting, a setting for one, or just a cup, plate or serving piece, depending on the agreement set forth. And just like in grocery stores today, the completing pieces back then were extra. If you wanted the butter dish for your set, it would have to have been purchased, because it was not part of the punch card agreement. Because of this, most of these extra pieces to complete a set were not purchased, and for that reason those pieces are much harder to find now and will be more expensive to today's collectors.

Elegant glassware of the depression era is a little different story. This glass was mostly mouth blown, handmade, shaped, and formed. Many of these already costly pieces were then given elaborate etchings. Master craftsmen would hand cut some of these etchings, using special grinders with copper cutting wheels, and many were made to specific order for excited brides who wanted their own special design or monogram. Some of these master craftsmen would go around the country setting up for well advertised freelance work at the larger high end stores such as Marshall Field's in Chicago.

But the most desirable etchings sought today, and for the past few decades, were those created by placing an etching plate or stencil over the piece, and brushing it with an acid, or submersing the piece into an acid bath that would eat into the glass and leave the design after the acid was rinsed away. To keep the acid from eating away at the whole piece of glass that was being etched, the areas that were not to be etched would have been covered with bee's wax.

Try to imagine how many people were involved in the process of making just one piece of elegant or handmade glass back in the depression era. I may be off a little bit, but I believe the number of workers for an undecorated piece of glass was a minimum of thirteen, and could run as high as twenty-one. Now, add in the finishing (etching, cutting, or hand painting) department, and I think you'll get the idea of the cost differences between machine made depression glass, and handmade.

Those fortunate enough to have money during the depression would not have the glassware that was given away at movie theaters and five and dime stores. These people would have their colored glassware from glasshouses that produced this much higher quality product. These wares would not be given away, but would be found at better department stores and even jewelry shops.

So while the Central Glass Works plant did make hotel and bar glassware, and it seems that is all they were really known for up to this point, as you will see, they produced some of the highest quality handmade glassware in the country. This is the glassware you will find in this reference.

Pricing glassware for this reference was difficult at best, and should not be the last word on prices. Prices will vary by region and market. Please note though, pricing will not be set by auctions, whether live, or those found in cyber space. All pricing on glassware in this book is for pieces that are "as manufactured," this means no damage, scratches or repairs of any kind.

# The History of Central Glass Works

The Works formed like a phoenix from the ashes of the Central Glass Company. During the United States Glass Company takeovers and attempted takeovers of the late 1880s, and into the 1890s (read more about this later), the giant U.S. Glass Company did manage to acquire the Central Glass Company, only to close it shortly thereafter, claiming labor troubles and lack of natural glass supplies motivated their decision. The plant remained closed for a few years. In 1895 former Central plant manager Nathan Bay Scott and some Wheeling businessmen put together enough capital to open the old plant back up. By 1896 the group and their employees started producing glass. Reusing the original company name was discussed but, instead, they decided on the name Central Glass Works. Although never really related to the original company, in later years we will see Central Glass Works refer to themselves as an ongoing part of the original Central Glass Company. It would appear that during tough business times the directors of the Works would play upon the history of the original company to attempt to revive the slumping market share or weak sales they were experiencing.

Tough times did plague the Central during their forty-four years, with a lack of protection from the federal government concerning inadequate tariffs on cheaper foreign products, natural gas shortages, and labor troubles. Natural gas was in short supply off and on in Wheeling, making it difficult to keep the furnaces running. Occasional fires would close the plant, causing a lapse in production. There were several such interruptions in CGW's history and it is a wonder they were able to achieve the status they did.

While not getting much press about what they did manage to do, they were giants in the glass industry with heavy production being sent to Europe as well as their domestic sales. The reason not as much is known about their work is that their history has not been written yet. Companies like Heisey, Cambridge, Tiffin, and Imperial all went out of business in the second half of the twentieth century and had more people around to help explain their past and write their stories. Their histories and files remained in one location during more prosperous times in our country, and this would make it easier to bring those stories to the surface, adding faces and names to the stories and events that made up such history.

Central Glass Works suffered from the fate of the Great Depression, and died out in 1939 during the worst economic times this country faced, trading a strong command of the glass market for a weak and quiet disappearance that could or would not even qualify as a small funeral. From a small blurb in the *Crockery and Glass Journal*, March 1940, we read,

> The equipment of the Central Glass Works, Wheeling W. Va., was acquired by the Imperial Glass Corp., who will transfer most of it to Bellaire, Ohio, where this plant is situated. With the purpose of creating a "Central Glass Division," former employees of this company have been hired to produce the glass. According to Carl W. Gustkey, chairman of the board of directors of Imperial, this new division will be put into operation within two, three months. G.C. White of Wheeling purchased the Central equipment as a private individual, reselling it to Imperial.

We know that the purchase by G.C. White must have taken place in the latter part of 1939, but who was he and what was his reason for making the purchase to begin with?

More important unanswered questions on Central's history exist such as, where did all the molds and etching plates end up? As more information is released on Central, I'm hoping it will force out more of the archives explaining the fragments of the details we are missing, i.e. those vital missing links!

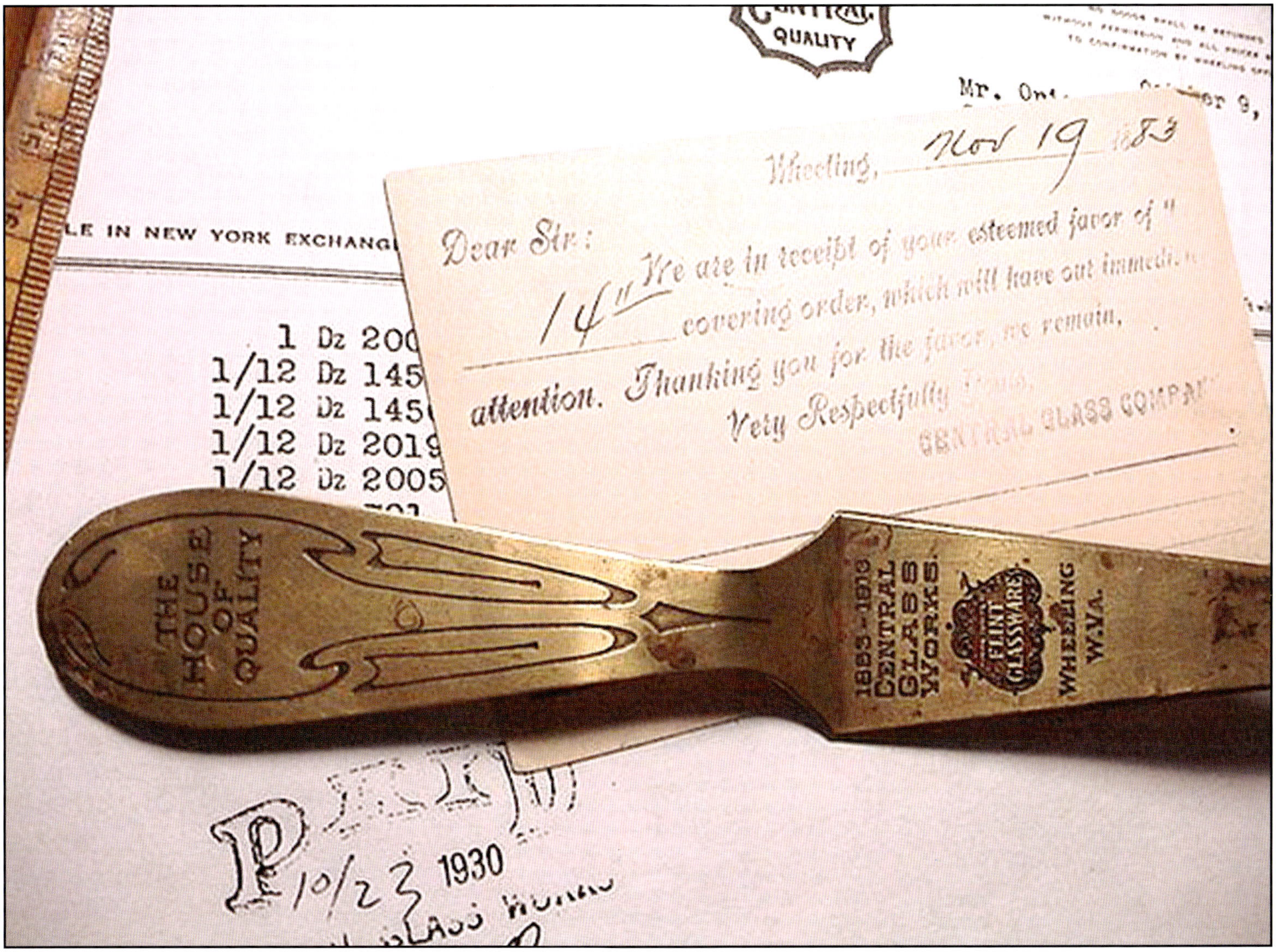


Central Glass Works letter opener claiming the company's roots to 1863. 9" long, dated 1863-1913, $250-$300.

# The Colors of Central Glass Works

While Central made all of the colors we came to expect in glass of the period, there are trade journal excerpts that lay claim to Central pioneering the Rose (pink) colored glassware. Central also claims in a press release to have originated the luncheon plate. Colors and variations of Rose, Green, Amber, Blue, Electric Blue, Black, Opal, Clambroth, Vaseline, Limelight, Canary, Heatherbloom, Amethyst, Pamona Green, various fired on colors, and satin finished examples made up their rainbow of colors. In 1928 the very glamorous Orchid Tints was added, and in 1931, Golden Sapphire was introduced. Possibly the best looking glassware made by the Central is colored with their Golden Sapphire and Orchid Tints colors. Central also did cased glass as well as gold encrusting work. While some of the gold treatment work done by Central is flawless and equals that of Pickard of Chicago, there exists examples of Central's wares where the gold is done terribly. I am hoping that we'll find out down the road a bit that these lesser quality wares were in fact bought as discounts from possibly an outlet shed, or were in fact bought as etched pieces and gold treated by another finisher.

Stretch (iridescent) Glass and Art Glass were also made at the Central Glass Works plant during the 1920s and '30s, and are of the highest quality. The Stretch lines are often confused with that of the Dugan Diamond and Fenton Art Glass companies, while their Art Glass lines are comparable to items made by Stueben and Pairpoint.

# Trademark Logos

We know the Central Glass Works logo that reads The Old Central Quality was adopted from the Rochester Tumbler Company's logo that read The Old Rochester Quality. This style of trademark will be used just after 1908, and can be found on foil as well as paper stickers when found on examples of Central's wares. Somewhere along in the next few years, the word The was dropped from the logo and it became simply, Old Central Quality. These stickers will be found this way on foil as well as paper and are found with black backgrounds and gold lettering.

The other logo is the round paper style, and when found on glass pieces has a blue background with white lettering. Shown in this logo is the Chippendale tall compote with the words **Central Glass** in the center. On top in the circle it reads **Trade Mark**, in the bottom **Wheeling W Va**. It is believed that CGW used both trademarks up to their closing, and no pieces have been found that have actually carried a signature or signed etching in the glass itself, other than the Krys-Tol trademark on the Chippendale line.

If you have a piece of glass that has a sticker that reads, Central Glass, and it is not as above, it's not from this company. Please read the section entitled Other Companies Named Central Glass later in this reference.

Central Glass Works trade mark label "Old Central Quality."

Central Glass Works trade mark logo, blue & white.

Central Glass Works trade mark label "Old Central Quality" on Etch 10 Thistle, St. Regis Tumbler, tumbler w/ sticker $45/80.

Central Glass Works trade mark logo "Krys-Tol.".

# The Line Numbers

What I would like to do is give you **all** of the line numbers ever produced by Central Glass Works from just after 1900 up to their closing, but I don't know them all, either because we have not found them yet, or those that hold the catalogs are not willing to share that information. So, you'll get what we know at this time. I have been told by a pretty wise person that if I wait until I know everything there is to know about Central Glass Works, I would more than likely not live to share this information. So here's what I can tell you at this time.

What follows are known factory line numbers for the products manufactured by the Central during the depression era. Mostly we will have images of, being real examples, scanned trade journal copies, catalog copies, or line drawings to help explain the line. Now, let's go on and prove that Central Glass Works was not just a hotel and barware glassmaker, as the writings in history to this point would have you believe.

Catalog copy cover shot. *Author's Catalog*

Catalog copy cover shot. *Author's Catalog.*

# #43 Tumbler Line

### Colors: rose, green, and crystal with rose or green foot

Whenever these pieces are seen with the straight optic and clear with green foot (as the catalog states), they usually are referred to as unmarked Hazel Atlas products. While the glass is a much better quality, examples as such do not hold much desire for collectors. You will see glass buyers picking up pieces when they have the diamond or pineapple optic, or are in earlier produced color combinations not shown in this 1928 catalog copy. The catalog copy also states goblets and other stems, but they unfortunately do not show an example of those. On an interesting note, Central has made many references to the 2-3/4 ounce tumbler as being a Grape Juice Tumbler. In this catalog reprint they call it a Grape Juice or Orange.

#43 2-3/4 oz. Juice 3" tall tumbler, straight optic $4-8, diamond optic $8-18.

No. 43

WHEREVER the beauty of colored glassware is appreciated, the offerings illustrated above in green feet and either diamond or straight optic bowls will be welcome. The set includes Footed Tumblers in the following sizes: 2¾ oz., 4 oz., 6 oz., 9 oz. 10 oz. 11 oz., and 12 oz. Sherbets—both high and low stemmed—Ices, Goblets, Cocktail Glasses, Parfaits, Small Grape Juice or Orange Tumblers and Table Tumblers.

#43 line. *Author's Catalog* .

#43 6 oz. - 4-1/4" tall tumbler, straight optic $4-8, diamond optic $8-18.

#43 12 oz. 6-1/8" tall water tumblers, straight optic $4-8, diamond optic $8-18.

## #67 and #62 Line Compotes

**Colors: rose, green, crystal and decorated.**

#67 is the line number for the tall-footed compotes (or comports) and #62 is the number for the low footed ones. The #67's both measure 6-inches tall, the smaller one measures 5-inches across the top while the bigger one measures a full 6-inches. These are some of the most beautiful examples of Central's work. So large, yet so light and delicate, it makes people nervous picking an example up or handling it at all. One important thing to point out is all of these compotes are ground at the factory after the bust off is cut away. I have seen buyers pass these up because they thought they were ground down too far. That's the way they are so don't be afraid of them. The three shorter comports in the #62 line measure 4-1/2-inches, 6-inches, and the largest comes in at 7-inches across the top. These are much more durable than the taller cousins.

Rose colored #67 Compote, 6" tall, 6" wide across top, $50-75.

Rose & green colored #67 Compotes, 6" tall, 5" wide across top, $50-75.

## #210 Stem Line

While wanting to stay with Central's depression era works, adding previously unknown or improperly attributed items, such as the #210 line, will keep from attributing these items to other glass companies. The example shown was purchased at a local flea market for eight dollars. This is the only one I have seen like it. The bowl and foot are blown and the stem molded and then appears to have been cut. Manufactured in the early 1900s, this high quality stem finds a place now in history.

CENTRAL GLASS WORKS,

WHEELING, W. VA.

210 LINE.—Design Patent [illegible]

Leading Manufacturers of Pressed and Blown Bar Goods.

Cut and Etched Lead Blown Tumblers and Stemware.

Fine Cut Bar Bottles, Decanters, Water Bottles, Bar Novelties.

—SALESROOMS:—

New York, 66 West Broadway. John H. Dobbs.
Chicago, 311 Garden City Block. H. E. Waddell.
Baltimore, 23 S. Charles St. Green & Seeman.
Philadelphia, 619 Arch St. Geo. R. Reinhart.

Trade journal reprint #210 line stem.

#210 Line wine stem, needle etched, 4-3/4" tall, 3 oz., $8-10.

# #284 Marmalade

### Crystal

I think a couple of words are necessary about the marmalade jar set which may keep you from buying a similar product incorrectly, although you may think you are actually getting this CGW marmalade. The jar measures 3-3/16-inches tall, 2-11/16-inches inner diameter, and the base curves upward slightly on the underside. The top is notched for the spoon and has a shouldered lip that fits comfortably down in to the jar, measuring about 5/16 of an inch. The #283 Coaster/Liner measures 4-1/4-inches across and not 4-1/2-inches as the catalog states and it stands over 3/4 of an inch high. It will only be found with the round knob finial shown in the example. Watch for mismatch marriages to improper liners where someone will have substituted an ashtray or coaster.

#284 Marmalade, cover, spoon, and liner plate, see article for measurements. Without etch: $50-75.

# #500 Covered Candy

### Colors: ebony, green, rose, & amber

This is the cone footed candy jar that has been most commonly called a Tiffin Product. Not only is it close to Tiffin, it's also similar to Westmoreland, Cambridge, Fenton, and New Martinsville. Everybody made this style of covered candy and the bottoms are very hard to tell apart except for color. The tops will all vary in the angle of the glass from the finial to the rim and the finial itself will be shaped slightly different, or be different in height. Central's blank (a "blank" is the term or name for an individual product line) top and bottom is a two-part mold and measures exactly 7-1/2-inches tall assembled. The lid, from the flat level surface to the top of the finial, measures 3-inches. The candy bottom has a top rim outer diameter of exactly 6-inches with a single disc separator and an inverted cone foot. The foot outer diameter measures 3-3/8-inches. This should help keep you from unintentionally buying a married piece.

#500 Line candy and cover, see article for measurements. Without etch: $50-60.

# #700 Stem Line

#700 Line of stemware, trade journal reprint.

### Crystal only

Another line number from the early 1900s is the 700. If you keep in mind that the plant was destroyed by fire in 1901 and the inventory quickly sold off, the plain fact is that any of the lines found today that survived from this era must have been well protected. Lines sold in bulk after the fire may have gone to restaurants, hotels or cruise lines. I have never seen this line in person but wanted you to see this reprint in case you find some. Remember while looking at the ad reprint from the trade journal, though while the images may look gray and dull, the metals content will have been of the highest quality. These stems should sparkle with near the brilliance of cut crystal. Looking like Morgantown or Tiffin products it will be nice to have them take their rightful place in glass history.

# #780 Stem Line

### Colors: green, rose, crystal and combinations of crystal and colors (should be found in amber)

The 780 blank is similar to many other companies that used this type of pulled stem. With Central's example, the wide part of the stem seems to be closer to the bowl than with that of other makers. There are nine sizes listed in the catalog and three are shown here. Something else worth mentioning is that every **tall** saucer champagne I have seen or owned has been polished or cut down to the height shown in the example. I am given to believe that this was done at the factory to control the size, shape, and look for this particular stem. I'm mentioning this so you do not turn away from the stem thinking it has been ground. The factory measurements for this stem and others in this line are listed below. This process of production is also evident on the #67 line of compotes and the product may have been hard to flame polish due to breakage. The base may be found with cut rays on the underside.

| **Item** | **cap.** | **height** | **top dia.** | **base dia.** | **crystal** | **green/ rose** |
|---|---|---|---|---|---|---|
| Cordial | 3/4 oz. | 4-7/16 | 1-9/16 | 1-11/16 | | |
| Saucer champagne | 6 oz. | 5-11/16 | 3-15/16 | 2-15/16 | $10-12 | $12-15 |
| Tall saucer champagne | 6 oz. | 6-1/2 | 4 | 3 | $10-12 | $12-15 |
| Sherbet | 5-1/2 | 4-1/4 | 3-3/4 | 2-13/16 | $6-8 | $10-12 |
| Water goblet | 9 oz. | 7-5/8 | 3-3/4 | 3" | $15-18 | $22-25 |

#780 Water goblets 7-5/8" tall crystal $6-18 Colors $10-25.

#780 tall saucer champagne, 6-1/2" tall, $10-15; sherbet, 4-1/4" tall, $6-12.

# #1103 Line

### Colors: green, amber, crystal and rose, crystal with cased green, orange, & purple, gold bands or trim with various etch designs, and wheel cut

The only known pieces so far in this line are cheese and cracker sets, consisting of a large round plate with a raised indent for the cheese comport or dish, or a small round covered box. Keep in mind that although not illustrated here the liner plate is also found with a rayed base. Also, it's worth mentioning that the liner plate is cupped or bowl-shaped almost to the point of being able to double as a soup bowl. The cheese dish has a measurement of 2-3/4-inches high with a 4-5/8-inch flared rim measured at the outside diameter. The plate measures 1-1/4 high and 9-1/2-inches in diameter and weighs over a pound and a half. The round covered box I'm going to guess is about 3-inches high and fits perfectly in the indented ring of the tray. These are guesses because I've never seen this box in person. Many or most companies made a cheese and cracker set, but nothing quite like the product produced by the Central. There is a picture of the 1103 cheese and cracker tray in the catalog shot along with the 2000 line. I would consider the representative set shown below to be part of Central's Art Glass Line.

#1103 cheese & cracker tray, see article for measurements, $15-65 depending on color or treatment.

#1103 cheese & cracker tray showing ruby center and foot.

## #1316 Stem line

**Colors: crystal rose, green & amber**

To date this would appear to be a very small stemware line consisting of less than a half dozen sizes, the 9 oz. goblet, 6 oz. saucer champagne, 6 oz. low sherbet, 3 oz. wine, and 1 oz. cordial. The bowls of the goblets are blown and set over pressed stems with a nice wide seat for the bowl to sit on. The foot will also be blown and shaped to size. While the water goblet, wine, and cordial share the narrow V-shape bowl, the champagne and sherbet will have a wider shaped bowl, but still remains V-shaped.

#1316 wine and cordial, $6-10.

## #1317 / 167 Vase (flared top)

**Colors: rose, green, amber, orchid tints, black, amethyst and crystal**

This is the line number given to the cigar-shaped vase that has had the top neck area narrowed and the lip area flared outward and tooled or crimped while hot. It measures approximately 10-inches tall and will come in all regular or normal colors as well as decorated and/or etched. Although not as recognizable as the cigar-shaped counterpart previously made famous, this piece was much more labor intensive to produce. While I have no example to show, looking at the vases in the following chapter one can imagine how it would look with the neck area pulled in and the top lip flared outward and crimped to the desire of the finisher performing the task.

## #1320 / 168 Vase (cigar shape)

**Colors: rose, green, amber, black, orchid tints, amethyst, and clear**

The infamous cigar-shaped vase that for decades has been called Tiffin, or Morgantown's Luna, finally gets its due as the line number has finally come to light. It measures 10-inches tall and will be found in all the normal colors as well as being treated with any number of decorations or highlights. Prices will vary by color and any gold highlights or decorations.

#1320/168 cigar vases, 10" tall, $15-60 depending on treatment and color.

# #1422 Line

### Colors: rose, green, amber, and crystal with color combinations

This is one of Central's pressed lines, or pressed with blown bowl combinations. None of the pieces found without an etch command high prices except for the cigarette holder. Items can be found in plain, paneled or diamond optic. Prices are for blanks with no etching. These stems were also made later by Imperial Glass after the company's acquisition of Central and into the 1950s, and some of those later stems are found with a bit of extra glass on the lip area.

#1422 line trade journal ad copy.

#1422 wafer separator stem goblet, 6-1/8" tall, $10-15.

#1422 wafer separator stem sherbet, 4" tall, $10-15.

#1422 wafer separator stem cigarette holder, $25-45.

# #1426 Line

## 1920s, early '30s: rose, green, and combinations of crystal and color. Candles in rose, green, amber, black, and crystal

Adding the following to this reference should stop all of these stems being referred to as Tiffin. This will be another of the lines shared between the two glass houses where both produced the same product. A great addition is finding a catalog copy attributing this line to Central, when we have only to this point seen it in Tiffin catalogs. So, is this a direct steal between the two houses? You know, I'll never believe that. Even more interesting though is finding this stem in a Bryce catalog dated 1916. So three companies made this same stem which means you will have to know the colors your company made as far as Tiffin or Central, but I'm sure the Bryce line would have only been made in crystal at that time.

Prices for the stems remain rather constant regardless of which company produced them. Combinations of crystal and colors are found but I have never seen an example in crystal only but believe because of the Bryce additions it does exist. They will be found with or without the diamond optic. Below are the sizes shown in the catalog copy. What does not seem to have been shared or made by other glass houses are the candlesticks in this line, which are found in two different heights. The shorter sticks measure 3-3/4-inches tall with a base diameter of 4-3/8, the taller measuring at 8-inches. The stem of the candle is spiral-shaped with a dual beveled separator half way down the stick. It's also noted that this blank was made from a three-part mold.

## All color combinations or crystal

| Item | capacity | height | price |
|---|---|---|---|
| Saucer champagne | 6 oz. | 6" | $9-20 |
| Water goblet | 10 oz. | 7-1/2 | $10-20 |
| Parfait | 6 oz. | | $10-20 |
| Sherbet | 6 oz. | 5-1/2 | $9-20 |
| Wine | 3 oz. | 5 1/2" | $15-20 |
| Tankard | | | $45-75 |
| Candles | | 4" | $25-35 |
| Candles | | 8" | $35-50 |

#1426 line catalog copy *Author's Catalog*.

#1426 cord stem, $9-20.

#1426 low candlestick, $25-35.

# #1428 Line

## Late 1920s, early 1930s: rose, green, amber, and orchid tints

Without a doubt this is one of the best looking lines Central ever manufactured, and the most highly prized by avid collectors. The factory name for the amethyst color is Orchid Tints.

Collecting this pattern without an etch will be difficult but not impossible. While there is not much of this company's works readily available, now and again some of the items do come onto the market and smart collectors do not quibble with price. Pitchers and tumblers are elusive to say the least while some stems can be found. If you are going to collect patterns by CGW, be prepared to be patient. The decanter will soar in price over its current value shown here as collectors of other Central patterns attempt to find stoppers for their etched pattern decanters. Also the scarcity of etched pieces will cause the plain blanks to be grabbed up by collectors to fill the void of missing pieces. The decanter with shot glasses and tray can still be found together.

| **Item** | **capacity** | **price** |
|---|---|---|
| Bowl fruit salad | | $45 |
| Decanter w Stopper | | $175 |
| Goblet cordial | 1 oz. | $45 |
| Goblet cocktail | 3 oz. | $45 |
| Saucer champagne | 6 oz. | $35 |
| Goblet water | 10 oz. | $55 |
| Goblet wine | 3 oz. | $45 |
| Pitcher | 2 qt. | $175-200 |
| Tumbler whiskey | | $35-50 |
| Tumbler ftd. grape juice | 2 3/4 oz. | $30-32 |
| Tumbler ftd. juice | 7 oz. | $30-35 |
| Tumbler flat water | 10 oz. | $45-50 |
| Tumbler ftd. ice tea | 12 oz. | $45-50 |

#1428 line catalog copy, *Author's Catalog*.

No. 1428

THIS design of European antecedents presents such an attractive appearance in use that it has met with widespread acceptance wherever shown. This pattern includes the 2 quart Jug, Goblet, Saucer Champagne, Sherbet, Cocktail, Wine, Fruit Salad and Tumblers in 2¾ oz., 7 oz., 10 oz., and 12 oz. sizes. It is offered in optic and in Rose, Green, Amber and Orchid tints. The charm of this design fully meets the well known "Old Central" standards.

#1428 decanter, tray and shot glasses, *Author's Collection,* $275-350.

Tray for decanter set, 9-1/2" handle to handle, $25-40.

#1428 water goblet, 7-1/4" tall, $55; saucer champagne, 4-3/4" tall, $35; wine, 5-1/2" tall, $45.

No. 1434

A distinct novelty is featured in this line by the introduction of the festoon optic, a very pleasing departure from the conventional optic designs. This marks the line as something different and adds to the appeal to the hostess who seeks individuality in her table service. Offered in Rose, Green, Amber and Orchid, in all over tints. The line includes Goblet, Sherbet, Parfait, Cocktail and Wine.

#1434 line catalog copy, *Author's Catalog*.

# #1434 Line

### Colors listed: rose, green, amber, and orchid tints

This line has a short, squatty stem with hexagon separator. The pattern includes a goblet, sherbet, parfait, cocktail, and wine, and will be found with or without the festoon optic. An "optic" is the term used to define the treatment or effect performed on an otherwise plain piece of glass. A "festoon optic" would have a drape or pillowy look when finished. The separator between the bowl and the foot is similar to the 1440 as well as other Central lines.

You can see in the catalog reprint on the Central stem it has almost an equal distance between both halves of that separator. Shown in the photo is a very close stem, but the separator sits just under the bowl. I am hoping this etching is Central, but I have not found it in any catalog, and it's the only piece like it that I have found.

Unknown etch, possibly Central, almost similar stem, $20-25.

## #1435 Line

### Pastry Trays or Center Handled Servers: almost all colors and treatments

This is the line number for the round center handled servers and is one of the blanks that has carried over in years, originating from the Krys-Tol or Chippendale line. Prices vary for colored or etched, but plain crystal does not bring high prices. It is also found with elaborate cuttings. Factory image of the pastry tray will be found on two different catalog copies of the 2000 line. (See 2000-line information.)

#1435 pastry tray, $10-25.

## #1440 Line

### Colors: crystal, rose, green, and orchid tints

It is nice to have a line number for this stem after all these years. While tougher to find at the bigger shows, better finds can be made at smaller markets and antique shops. They are found in crystal, rose, and orchid tints, as solid colors, as well as combinations of crystal bowls with rose or green stems. The sizes are listed below as to what can be found. This is another stems only blank, so there are no dinner plates or serving pieces in the line.

No. 1440

WE present, with considerable pride, one of the most beautiful designs it has been our privilege to sponsor. Made in the new Orchid coloring as well as Crystal and Rose, and in Crystal bowls with rose or green stems. The 1440 line consists of Goblet, Saucer Champagne, Sherbet, Wine, Cocktail, Parfait, Fruit Salad, Grape Fruit and Tumblers in 2⅝ oz., 7 oz., 10 oz. and 12 oz. sizes.

**Left:**
#1440 line, *Author's Catalog.*

**Right:**
#1440 tall water goblet, 8-1/8" tall, $25-35.

#1440 saucer champagne, 6-9/16" tall, $25-35.

# #1445 Line

### Colors: rose, green, amber or combinations of colors and crystal

This is another one of Central's patterns that appears elusive. One theory on locating these hard to find pieces is, unless a seller can identify it and put a price on it, the piece will not hit their booths. So for years (and before the Internet), pieces that were unidentified were kept hidden in inventory, and if they made it to shows at all would usually remain in boxes under tables, leaving their limited sales space for more desirable and fast moving patterns. I state this as fact, as I have met a seller in St. Louis that has a score of unknowns he is sitting on, waiting for the correct identification of the pieces.

With the introduction of the internet and digital cameras, people are no longer taking their finds to dealers or antique shops, yet bringing these pieces right to market through web site auctions, as unknowns. Those searchers looking for the more obscure patterns not yet popularized by the depression glass annuals, will hunt the unknown categories of online auctions looking for these great finds.

The stem separator of this blank looks like a faceted cut jewel which does not contact the bottom of the bowl directly. There is a similar pattern that folks have sent me images of that is close to the 1445, but the jeweled separator on the look-a-like is in contact with the blown bowl at the base. Another way to tell the Central stem from others is where the stem meets the jeweled separator. On the 1445, the stem comes into the separator jewel straight in and straight out. On the look-a-like, the stem widens as it meets or blends into the jewel, and then blends back out going down the stem to the base.

The catalog reprint shows a full line of stems and a fruit salad bowl as well as the tumblers. Known pieces/sizes are shown in the catalog reprint. Although not listed in the catalog, there is a 10 oz. tumbler.

#1445 table tumblers, 12 oz., 5-9/16" tall; 10 oz., 5-1/8" tall, $15-25.

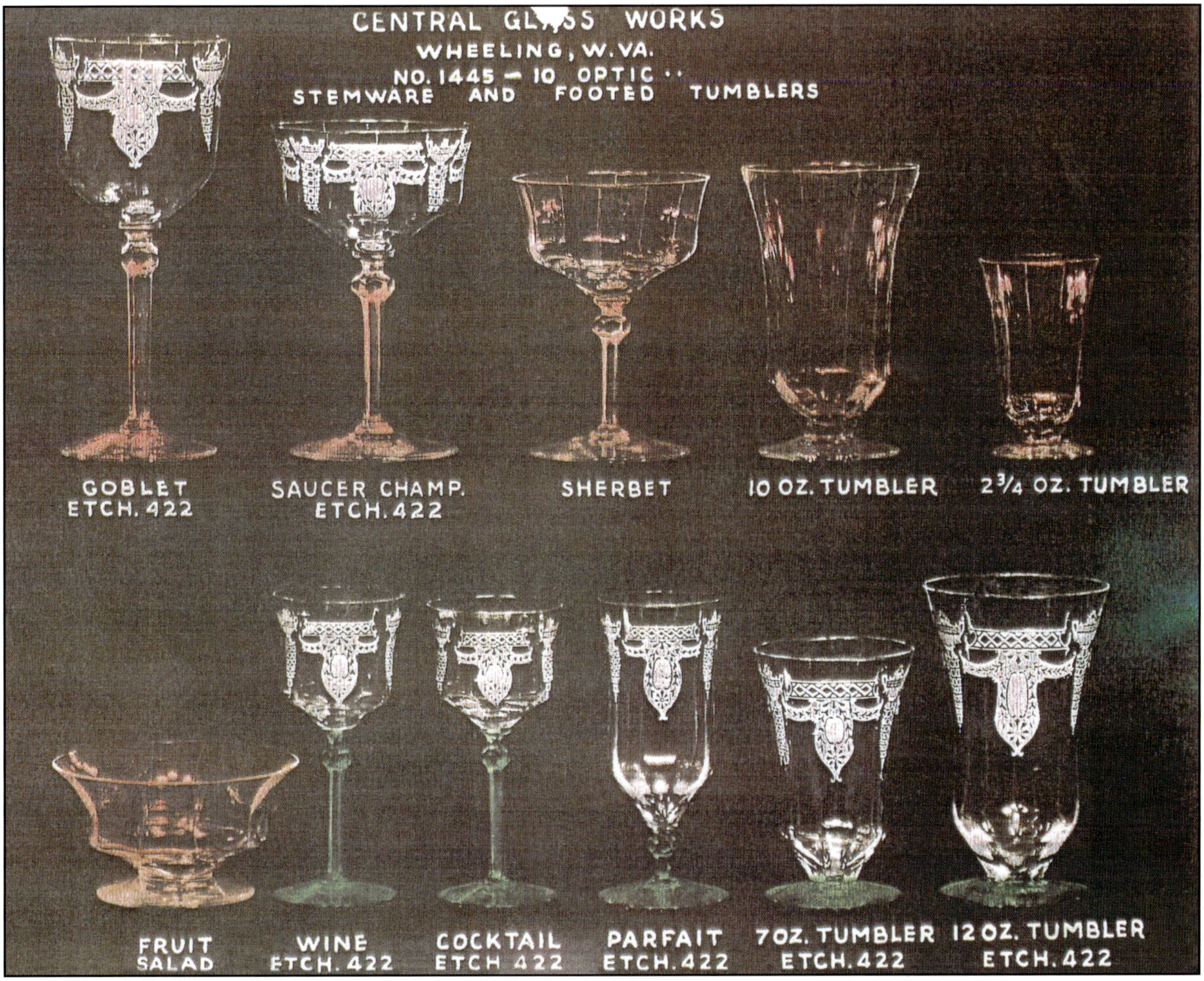


#1445 stem and tumbler line. *Catalog Copy Courtesy Dean Six.*

## #1446 Line

**Colors: rose, green, orchid tints, crystal, and color combinations including black.**

I've always heard this line referred to as Fostoria because of its close resemblance to two of their stemware lines. Fostoria made a similar stem on one line and a somewhat similar bowl on another. On the Fostoria line you will find it has a closer, or very narrow optic. There are more of the bellows or ribs in the blank and they're closer together, and this piece is usually found in yellow.

#1446 or Moderne wine, 3 oz., 5-5/8" tall; cocktail, 3 oz., 5" tall, $40-45.

Also, you may find a similar stem, but with the steps of the stem in a more teardrop shape. The corners of the steps are more rounded at the shoulders and there are less of these steps. I believe the similar stem only has four of the teardrop-shaped steps.

This is another stemware/tumbler only line but it does have a fruit salad bowl. Those folks looking for this nice deco pattern can find pieces, and prices of tumblers should not be out of reach. Stems on the other hand are priced like rarities because of the deco look of the line that appears timeless to collectors.

Long ago this line was given the name Moderne by Hazel Marie Weatherman, and that was due to the fact that the original sales releases or ads found in the glass house trade papers such as *China Glass & Lamps*, or *Crockery & Glass Journal*, advertised the line as, "Stemware In The Moderne Manner." Since CGW did not give this pattern a factory name and Hazel Marie did name it, that name will stick with this blank for all time, unless someone does eventually uncover a real factory name down the road somewhere.

Curiously, the #1470 line was also referred to in company ads as Stemware in the Moderne Manner, but was not given the same name.

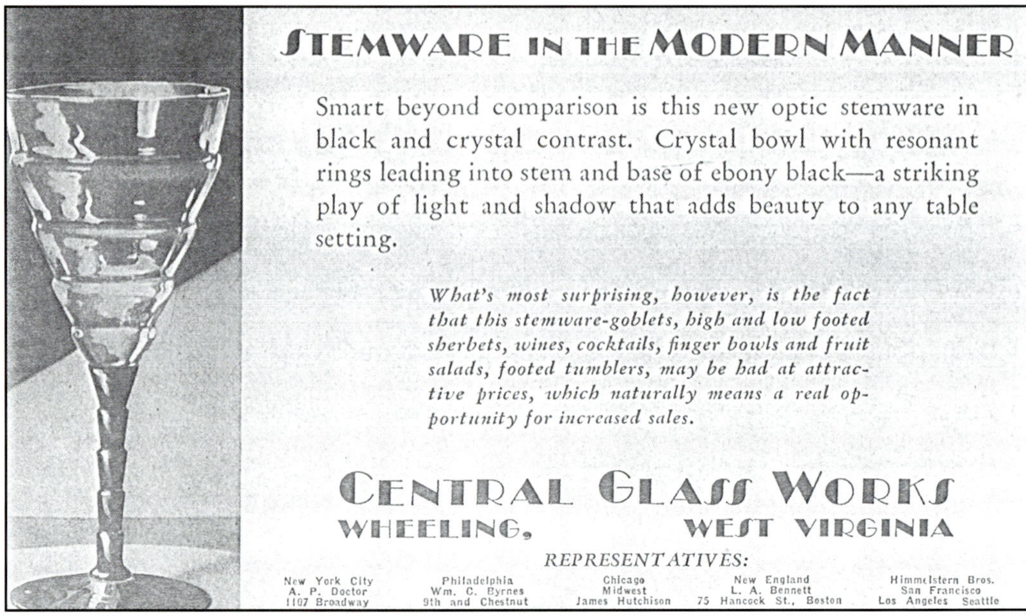


#1446 or Moderne, trade journal reprint.

#1446. *Catalog Copy Courtesy Dean Six.*

#1447 walnut stem water goblet, 10 oz., 8-1/8" tall, $25-40; champagne, 6 oz., 5-7/8" tall, $20-25.

# #1447 Line (Walnut Stem)

### Colors: golden sapphire, orchid tints, green, rose, blue, crystal, and combinations of crystal and colors

I have had the material on the 1447 stem line completed for years, and a 1447 stem recently shows up in Orchid Tints, proving again that no matter how much we believe we know (or it seems do not know) about this company since they closed their doors over sixty-four years ago, every day is a new learning experience.

This is the stem that looks like it has a walnut for a separator. The Heisey Glass Company had produced a line of glassware called Charter Oak, which has an acorn in the stem, and CGW had their walnut.

The line is comprised of five different stems, four different sized tumblers, and a fruit salad. That's it by the catalog, but I wouldn't be surprised in the future to find something different or additions to the line. As is the case with the rest of Central's work, it is not found too easily. Finds of this pattern, especially in Golden Sapphire, and now Orchid Tints, are the things Central hunters hope for.

Pieces listed are shown in the catalog copy below. Unable to price due to scarcity.

#1447 table tumbler, $15-18.
#1447 Walnut stem.

*Catalog Copy Courtesy Dean Six.*

# #1448 Line

**Colors: Crystal and combinations of rose and crystal, possibly crystal with combinations of green or amber may be found.**

The stem on this line is hex or six-sided as are the two separators. When you first pick up a stem in this style the first thing you may notice is how sharp, crisp or defined those fire polished separators feel. Very high quality in materials and craftsmanship are evident in this line.

It could be easy to confuse this pattern with CGW's 1455 line. In 1448 the bowls of both the tumblers and stemware are cone-shaped or have very straight lines. In 1455 the bowls are rounded (cupped-shaped) or curve to the stem, otherwise they are identical.

Listed in the catalog are five stems (as in most lines by this company), a footed fruit salad bowl, and six tumblers. It will be hard to tell you what these examples sell for, as they're not commonly found in my region.

#1448 wine, 3 oz., 5-1/2" tall, $25-35; tumbler, 8 oz., 5-1/8" tall, $15-18.

#1448 stem line. *Catalog Copy Courtesy Dean Six.*

# #1450 Line

**Colors: rose, green, black, amber, golden sapphire and combinations of crystal and colors, and colors over black foot, also plain crystal. Vases in rose, green, amber, and ebony with gold overlay.**

The plates and bowls in this complete tableware line are often confused with Fostoria's Mayfair pattern. While the 1450 line has three sharper pronounced peaks in each corner, the Fostoria pattern has bumps, more like rolling hills. There is also another line similar to the 1450 that has a group of small beads on the plates along the long stretch between the corners. While many hope this to be a Central blank because the corners are so similar, we have not found it in any Central catalog as such, but with the help of New Martinsville Guru, Robert Carlson, we did locate this particular line as being part of the New Martinsville line #36. Also, there is a line by Paden City that almost matches the sugar and creamer. See the Look-A-Like section to see them side-by-side.

The stemware in this line cannot be confused with any other manufacturer. The scalloped underside foot is Central's own. Keep in mind that the 1450 will have bowls that are rounded to the stem, unlike the 1451 line that has cone or V-shaped bowls, but have the same identical foot. Also interesting to note is the discovery of magnificent vases in this line, which do not appear in the catalog information.

| **Item** | **Capacity/ size** | **crystal** | **crys/ colors** | **Golden Sapphire** | **Black** |
|---|---|---|---|---|---|
| Bowl celery | 12-1/8 | $10-12 | $15-18 | $20-25 | $25 |
| Bowl grapefruit | | $8-10 | $8-10 | $10-15 | $22 |
| Bowl pickle | | $8-10 | $8-10 | $10-15 | $22 |
| Bowl div. relish | 12 1/8 long | $10-12 | $10-20 | $20-25 | $25 |
| Bowl vegetable | | $15-20 | $15-20 | $18-25 | $30 |
| Creamer | | $20-22 | $20-22 | $25-28 | $25 |
| Cup/saucer | | $22-25 | $22-25 | $25-30 | $38 |
| Plate bread | 6-1/2 | $6-8 | $6-8 | $10-15 | $18 |
| Plate salad | 7-1/2 | $8-10 | $8-10 | $15-18 | $18 |
| Plate lunch | 8-1/2 | $20-25 | $20-25 | $25-30 | $22 |
| Sugar | | $20-22 | $20-22 | $25-28 | $25 |
| Tray Cream & Sugar | | | | | $75 |
| Pastry Tray Centre Handle | | | $75 | $75 | |
| Stem cocktail | 2-1/2 oz. | $18-20 | $18-20 | $25-30 | |
| Stem oyster | | $18-20 | $18-20 | $25-30 | |
| Stem fruit salad | | $22-25 | $25-28 | $28-35 | |
| Stem hi-ball | 5" | $20-22 | $20-22 | $22-28 | |
| Tumbler | 10 oz. | $20-22 | $20-22 | $28-30 | |
| Tumbler | 12 oz. | $22-24 | $22-24 | $28-30 | |
| Sherbet | 4-1/16 | $18-20 | $18-20 | $25-30 | |
| Wine | 3 oz. | $20-22 | $20-22 | $30-35 | |
| Vase | 6"- 8" | $15-18 | $20-35 | | $75 |

#1450 line. *Catalog Copy Courtesy Dean Six.*

#1450. *Catalog Copy Courtesy Dean Six.*

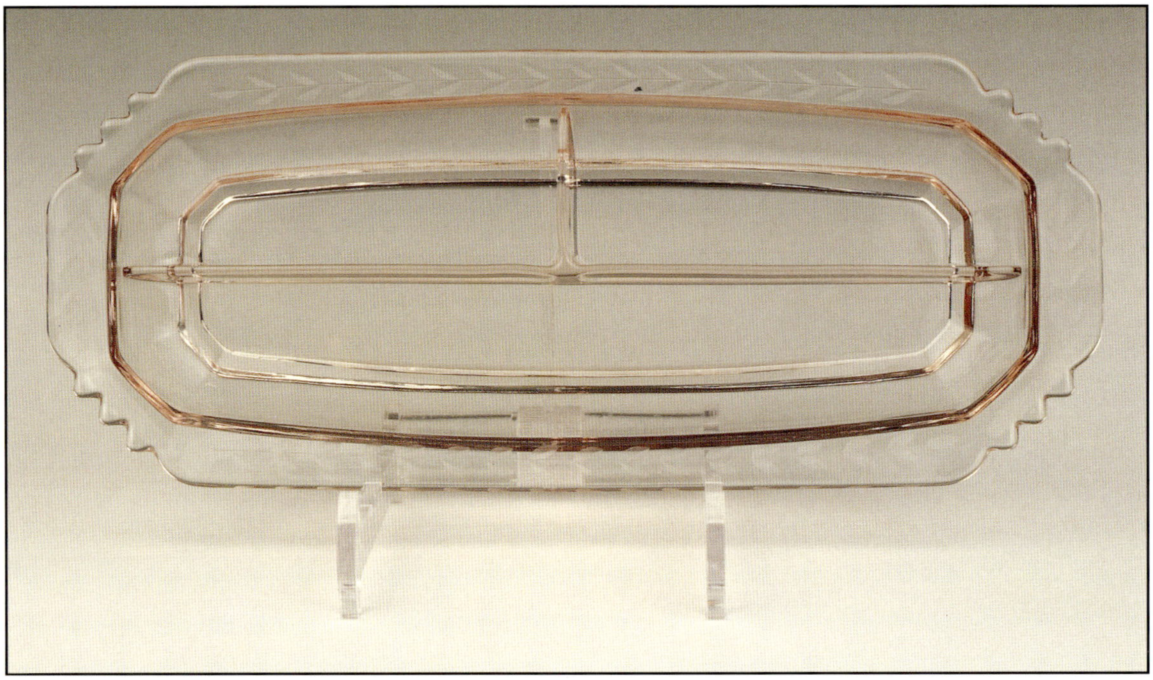

#1450 pink divided relish, 12-1/8" long, 1-3/8" tall, $10-20.

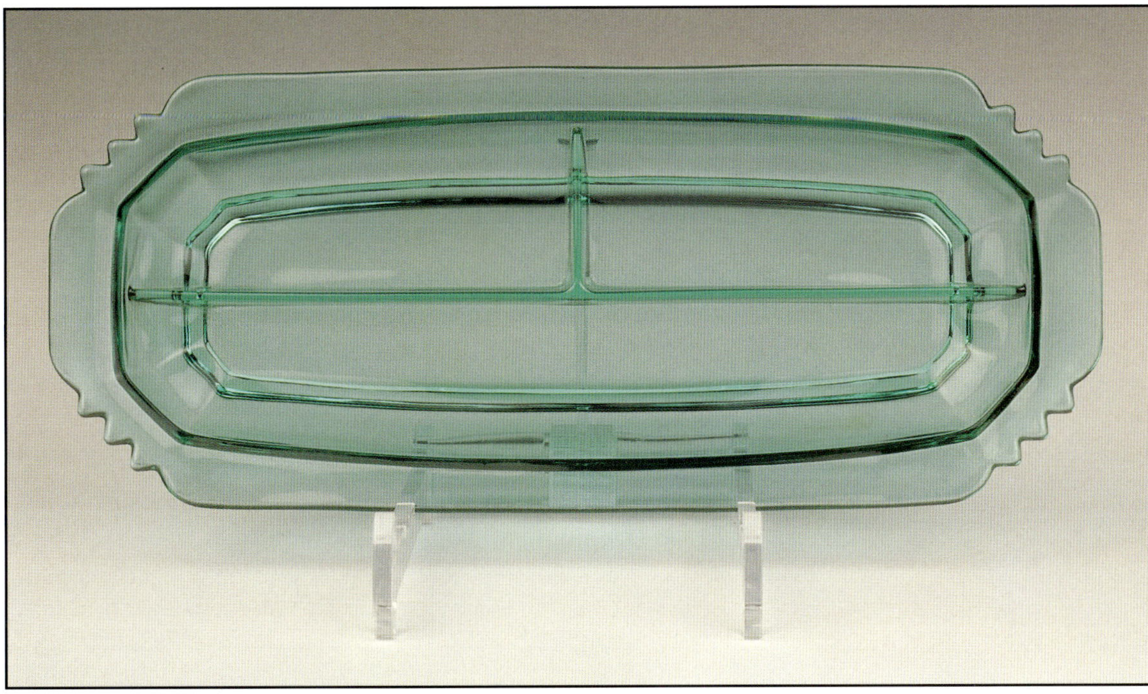

#1450 green divided relish, 12-1/8" long, 1-3/8" tall, $10-20.

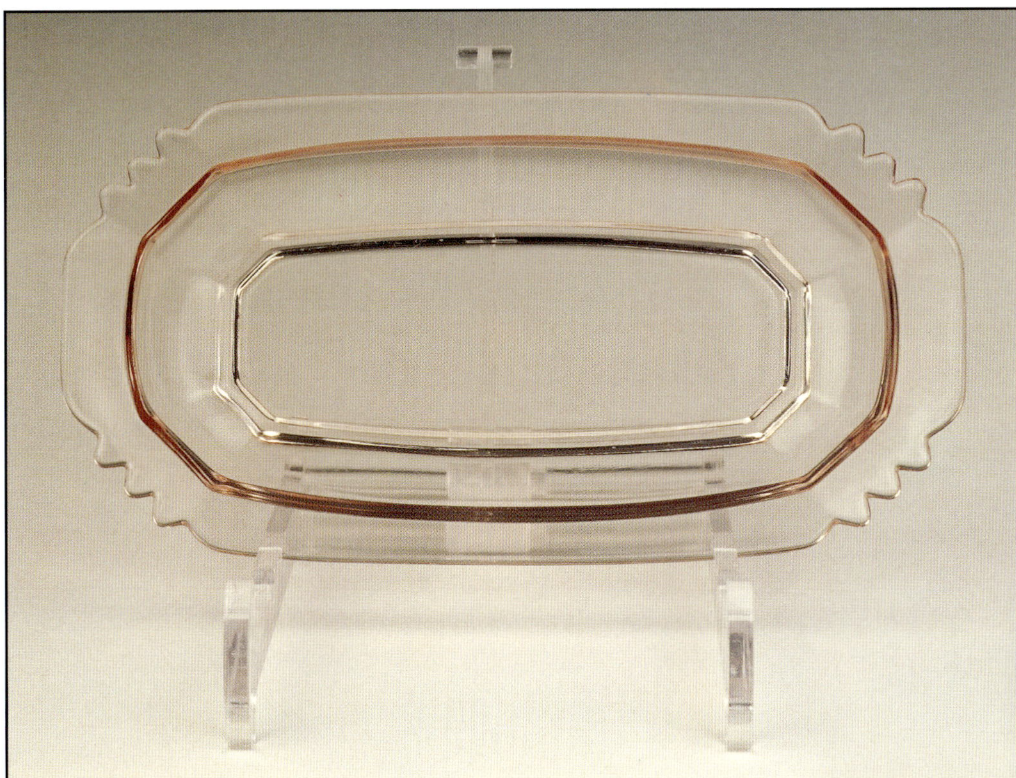

#1450 pink pickle dish, 7-7/8" long, $8-10.

#1450 green tumbler, 10 oz., 5-3/4" tall, flared lip, left side showing underside scallop of foot, $20-22.

#1450 crystal sherbet, 5-1/2 oz., 4" tall, *Courtesy Melissa Bratkovich*, $20.

#1450 pink and black sugar bowls, $20-22.

#1450 pink cup and saucer, $22-25; black cup and saucer, $35-38.

#1450 grapefruit bowl, 5-5/8" across, $22.

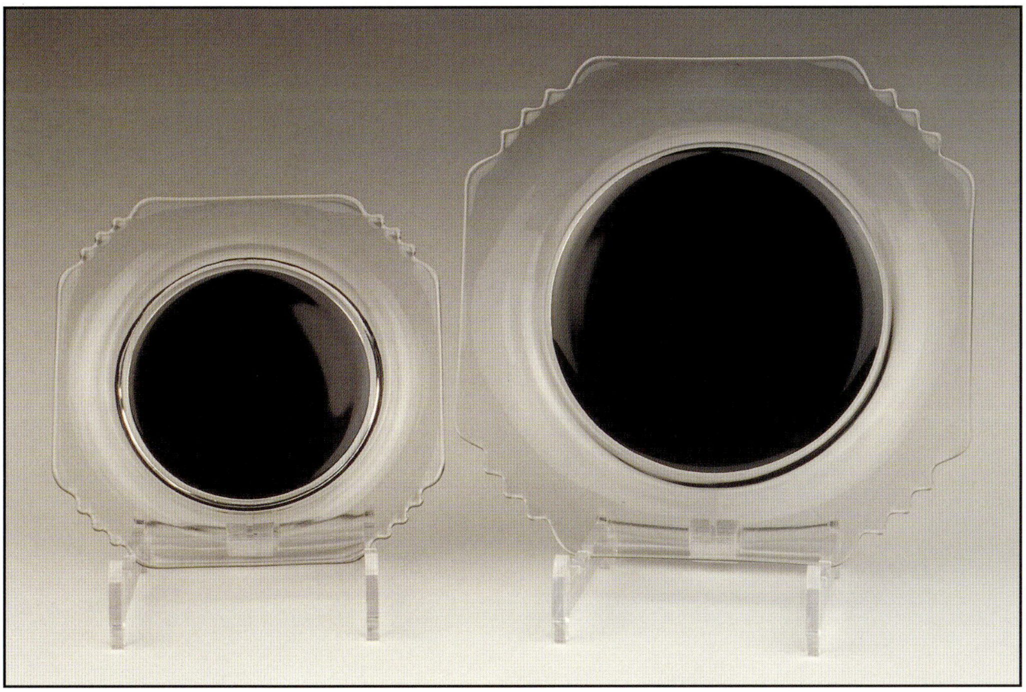

#1450 crystal & black, bread & butter, 6-1/2", $6-8; dinner plate, 8-1/2", $20-25.

#1450 black center handled server, $75.

#1450 black center handled server, top view, $75.

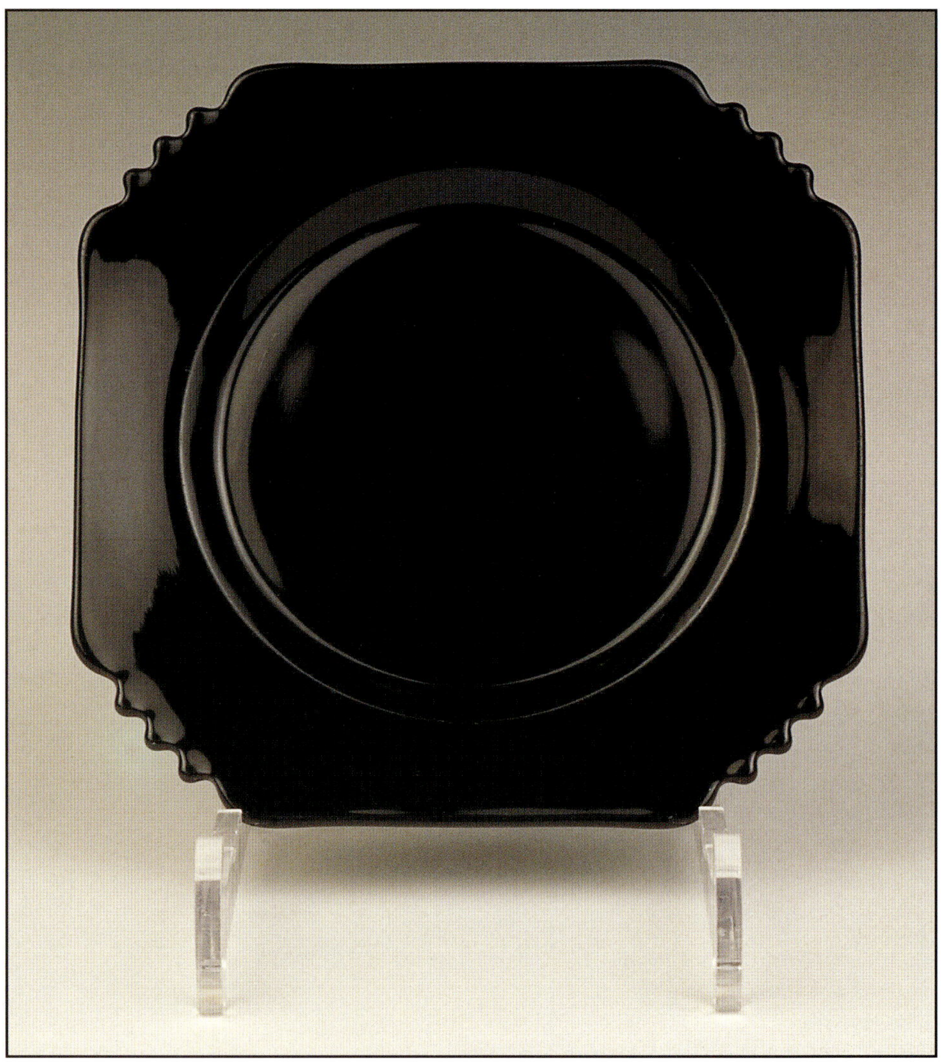

#1450 black plate, 7-1/2", $18.

#1450 ivy ball, *Photo Courtesy Larry Baker,* $125-150.

#1450 vase ebony and gold, Lovebirds design, *Photo Courtesy Lyle Fokken,* $150-175.

#1451. *Catalog Copy Courtesy Dean Six.*

# #1451 Line

**Colors: rose, green, amber, crystal, and combinations of colors.**

This line closely resembles the 1450 pattern. 1451 bowls are cone or V-shaped where 1450 bowls are rounded where they curve around to meet the base. Because of the elegant lines of this stem, it seems to be picked up fairly quickly if priced reasonably. There are only four stems in the line, and it would be easily compatible with the 1450 pattern without any trouble.

| Item | Crystal | Crystal/colors |
|---|---|---|
| Cocktail | $12-15 | $15-20 |
| Goblet | $15-20 | $18-22 |
| Sherbet | $15-20 | $18-22 |
| Wine | $15-20 | $18-22 |

#1451 sherbet, amber, 4" tall, $15-20.

# #1453 Line

### Colors: rose, green, amber, orchid tints, and combinations

This line of stems and tumblers is also not often found, yet. The line is comprised of six stems and four tumblers and on the catalog page they also show plates with a separate line number of 1384-1/2. Plate sizes are 6, 7, 8, 9 and 10-inch size. Blown bowls sit atop six-sided stems with an almost jeweled separator. There is a similar line folks have written to me about that needs to have the differences pointed out. On the 1453 stem, the jeweled or faceted separator sits right below the adjoining area of the bowl flange area with maybe a quarter inch gap. There is very little stem between the bowl and this separator. In the look-a-like, the separator is down 1/2-inch or so in the stem. Also coming away from the separator on the Central line, the stem comes out of the faceted nut from the middle. In the look-a-like, the stem starts to form from the outside (widest) lower part of the nut or separator, and likewise coming out of the separator it forms from the outside of the jewel. In Central's example, the stem comes out of the center of the jewel separator. Unfortunately, I do not have anything other than catalog images to show.

#1453 line. *Catalog Copy Courtesy Dean Six.*

# #1455 Line

### Colors: rose and rose & crystal combination

This pattern of stemware is another small line, there are only four pieces shown in the catalog. The stem and two separators are hexagonal and feel sharp to hold. Not dangerous mind you, but definitely not smooth to hold onto! The line consists of only the water goblet, saucer champagne, wine, and cocktail.

Prices should be pretty consistent across the line as there is usually not a lot of glamour in such small patterns that cannot be mixed with other similar lines. Keep in mind that this stem is also used on the 1448 line but those bowls are V-shaped, where the 1455 bowls are cupped-shaped. I have only seen this blank in Rose colored and Rose and Crystal combination.

#1455 Line saucer champagne, rose color, 6oz., 6-1/4" tall.

#1455 line. *Catalog Copy Courtesy Dean Six.*

# #1470 Line

### Colors: golden sapphire/crystal, rose, amber, green with crystal

One of Central's best, the quality of the glass used in this blank is fantastic, and the stem represents the true elegance of the era. This stemware is so beautiful in its design, that Imperial found themselves compelled to reissue the line in the 1950s. Most of those Imperial stems will be found with slightly thicker bowls and rim areas, and they will be more durable than the Central items made in the 1920s and '30s. However, I personally believe the glass Central made was of higher quality, even though more fragile or delicate.

The first thing you will realize when raising the stem is the raspy ball separator is sharp to hold too firmly, but not enough to be dangerous or cause concern.

The line is comprised of stems, tumblers, comports, and a footed fruit salad bowl, but was sold in compliment to sets of tableware in the 1450 line. Also, you will find more catalog images of the 1470 line in the etch #432 or Hester etch section.

| Item | capacity | height | rose/ green | amber | Golden Sapphire/ crystal |
|---|---|---|---|---|---|
| Goblet cocktail | 3-1/2 | 5-1/2 | $25 | $22 | $30 |
| Goblet cordial | 1-1/2 | | $35 | $35 | $40 |
| Goblet champagne | 6 oz. | 6-3/8 | $25 | $22 | $30 |
| Goblet parfait | 6 oz. | 5-1/2 | $30 | $28 | $38 |
| Goblet sherbet | 6 oz. | 4-5/8 | $25 | $22 | $30 |
| Goblet water | 10 oz. | 7-1/2" | $40 | $35 | $45 |
| Goblet wine | 3 oz. | 6-1/8 | $35 | $30 | $40 |
| Cocktail oyster | | 3-3/4" | $28 | $25 | $35 |
| Tumbler grape juice | 2-3/4 oz. | | $28 | $25 | $33 |
| Tumbler water | 7 oz. | | $28 | $25 | $33 |
| Tumbler water | 10 oz. | | $30 | $28 | $35 |
| Tumbler water | 12 oz. | | $33 | $30 | $40 |
| Tumbler whiskey sour | 4 oz. | 4-17/32 | | | |
| Compote | | 6-1/2" | $75-95 | | $125 |

#1470 sherbets, 5-1/2 oz., 4-1/2" tall, golden sapphire/crystal, $30; crystal crystal/colors, $15-25.

#1470 line. *Catalog Copy Courtesy Dean Six.*

#1470 cocktail, 3-1/2 oz., 5-1/2", crystal, $12.

#1470 compote, 6-1/2" tall, 7" across top, golden sapphire, $125 (without etch).

#1470 oyster cocktail, 3 oz., 3-3/4" tall, golden sapphire, $35.

#1470 saucer champagne crystal, 6-3/8" tall, (without etch) $20-25.

# #1820 Line Fan Vase

### Colors: green, rose and amber, orchid tints (possibly black as well as satin finished colors)

Due to the shape of these vases, and the fact that no two are the same, I believe these pieces started life a bit differently than the way they came out of their molds. The examples I have all vary in height, and all of the openings vary in width, proving they were formed by hand after they left their original molds. Where the mold seams run from the foot up the side of the vase, it will vary or turn away from its original line, in some cases quite a bit. It looks to be that the foot was held (like the Marie of a console bowl), as the fan area would be worked, sometimes twisting the upper area from the base while being formed. Also it seems that more than one worker or finisher was doing this job, as some vases twist clockwise from their base while others twist counterclockwise as if the workers were either left or right handed. Another thing that is noticeable is that the glass being very thick and obviously still very hot when worked, must have cooled too slowly for the weight of the mass as most of the vases are leaning from their base. Heights on the piece vary from just under 8-inches to 8-1/2-inches tall.

These vases, in fact, started their life rounded when just out of the mold, this being necessary for the plunger to move in and out of the mold. Therefore we can surmise that vases are totally hand-formed by finishers after being removed from the mold.

PICTURED above are a number of items which suggest themselves particularly at the time as gift ideas, bridge prizes, and for many other inexpensive gift requirements. The showing includes No. 2005 Lilly Bowl, No. 2005 Covered Relish, No. 2001 Flip Vase, No. 2007 7 inch Comport, No. 1820 Fan Vase, No. 2001 Cigarette Box and No. 2001 3-piece Mayonnaise Set. These pieces may be obtained in Green, Rose and Amber.

#1820 Catalog Copy C. 1928 various other lines also shown.

#1820 line fan vase, Orchid Tints, 8-1/2" tall, $75-90.

#1820 line fan vases, amber & rose, 8-1/2" tall, $30-45.

Winslow line, trade journal reprint.

## #1900 Line Winslow

### Combinations of crystal and colors, or plain crystal

The Winslow line, which is only comprised of stemware and made starting in 1937, though heavily produced, is still elusive to find. Pieces are of the best quality and come in crystal as well as combinations of crystal and rich colors. Bowls will be found in either plain or diamond optic. The colors of cobalt and ruby Winslow are exciting finds for Central collectors. This pattern would not be made available to the public, but rather would be part of the Hotel and Barware lines. Much appears to have found its way in to the public's hands though.

While usually confused with similar items made by Bryce, these stems spiral upward to the right from the base, where the Bryce products are just concentric rings.

Prices for Winslow should be moderate as is the case with most stemware only lines. If there is no complete tableware service, collectors will be limited to stem collectors, those who want to add them to their pottery dinnerware lines, and of course the Central aficionados. Prices have been seen from two to fifty dollars a piece with the latter being seen at shows, where dealers that knew the stems were Central were hoping they would bring that much. Sizes range from the small 3/4 oz. cordials to water goblets, and a total of thirty different pieces make up the line. I found the trade journal ad for Winslow interesting as Central rarely named their lines. Also enjoy the catalog copies, but note my sizes are actual measurements and they may be older examples than those of the transition period between Central and Imperial.

Winslow line cordial, green/crystal, 3/4 oz., 3-3/8" tall, $8-10; crystal brandy, 3/4 oz., 3-15/16" tall, $6-8.

Winslow cocktails, cobalt/crystal, 3 oz., 4-3/4" tall, $15-18; crystal side car, 4 oz., 4-1/2" tall, $6-8.

Winslow wine in ruby/crystal, 4-3/4" oz., 4-3/4" tall, $20-25.

Winslow, cobalt/crystal claret, 4 oz., 5-5/16" tall; sherry, 3 oz., 4-15/16" tall; wine, 3-1/2 oz., 4-13/16" tall, $15-18 each.

Winslow saucer champagne crystal, 5 oz., 4-3/8" tall, $10-12.

Winslow water goblet, 10 oz., 6-7/8" tall, $12-15.

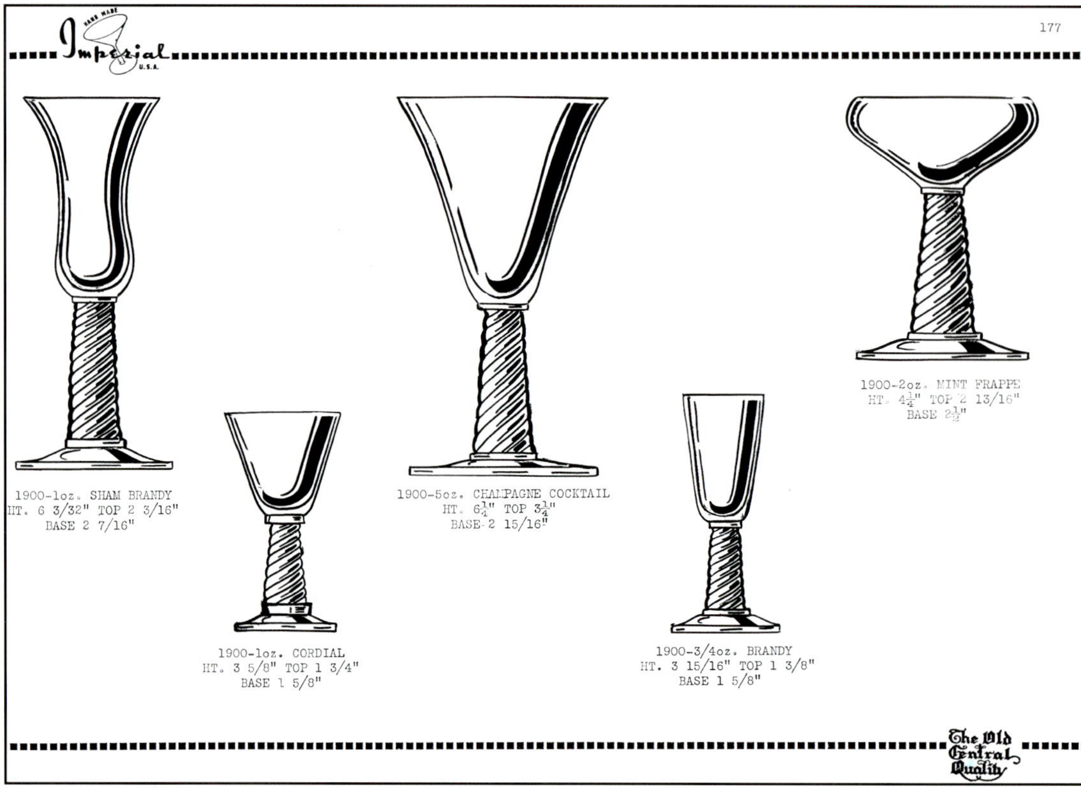


Catalog copy from 1939 Winslow #1900 line. *Author's Catalog.*

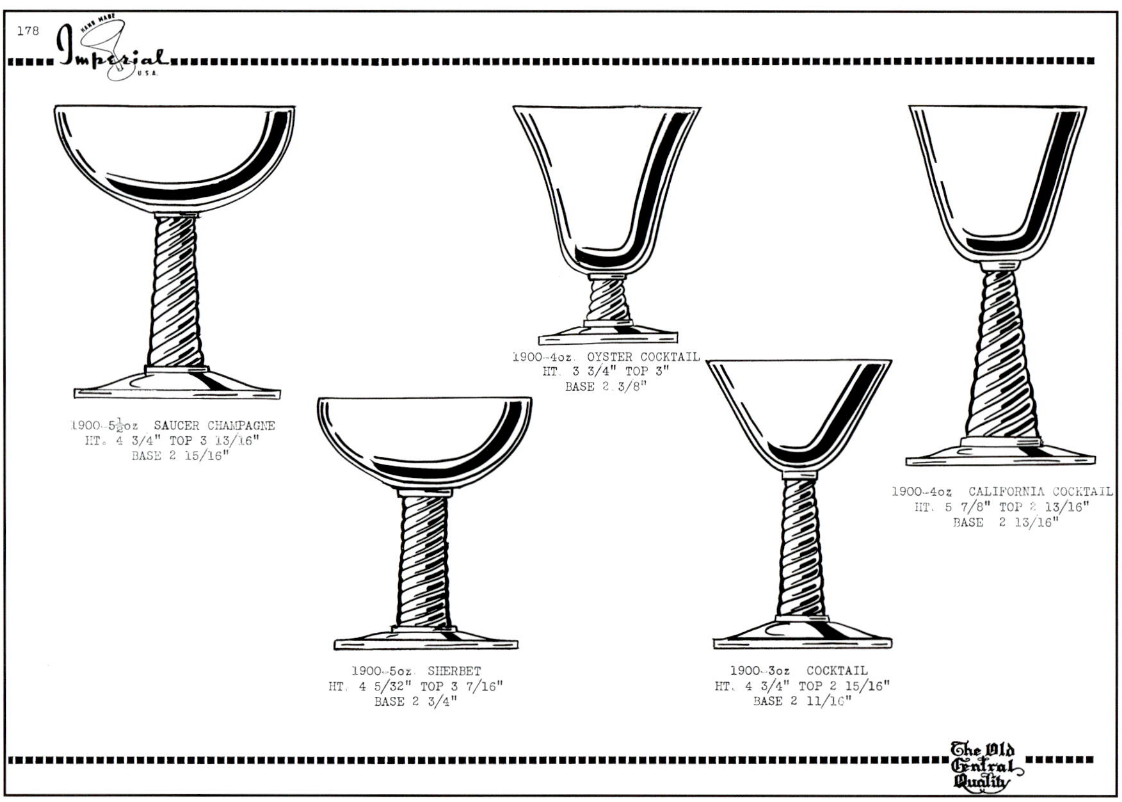


Catalog copy from 1939 Winslow #1900 line. *Author's Catalog.*

Catalog copy from 1939 Winslow #1900 line. *Author's Catalog.*

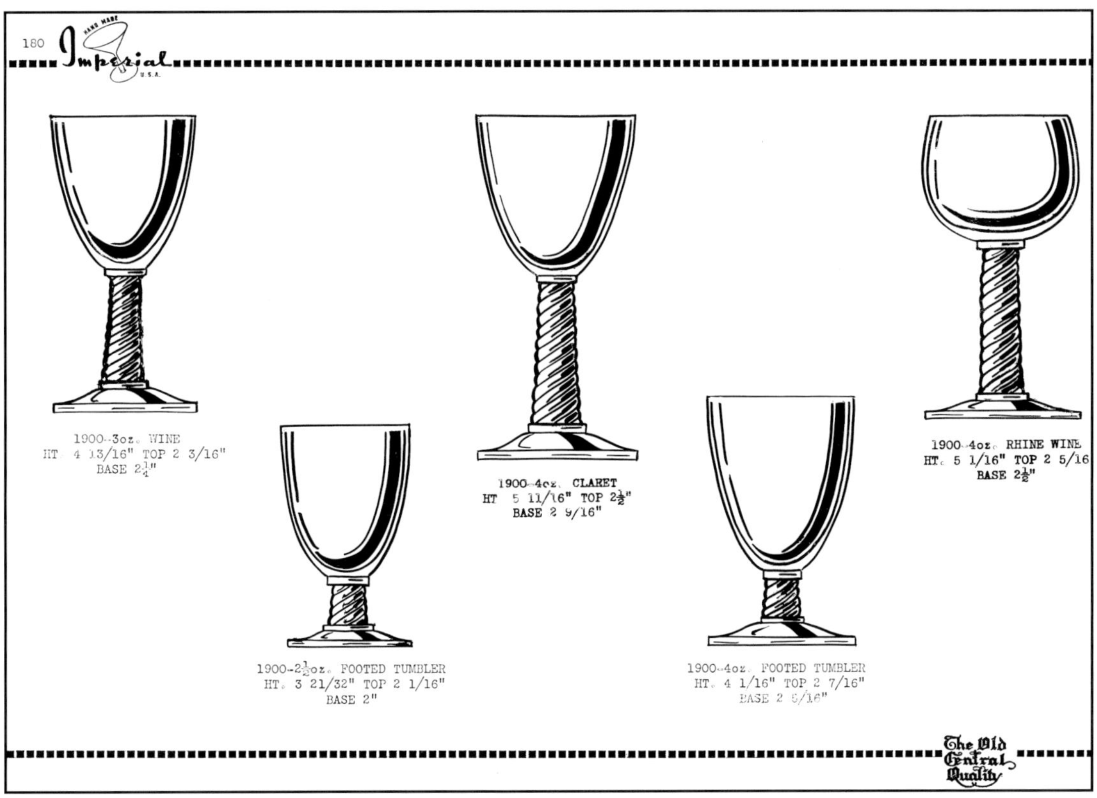


Catalog copy from 1939 Winslow #1900 line. *Author's Catalog.*

Catalog copy from 1939 Winslow #1900 line. *Author's Catalog.*

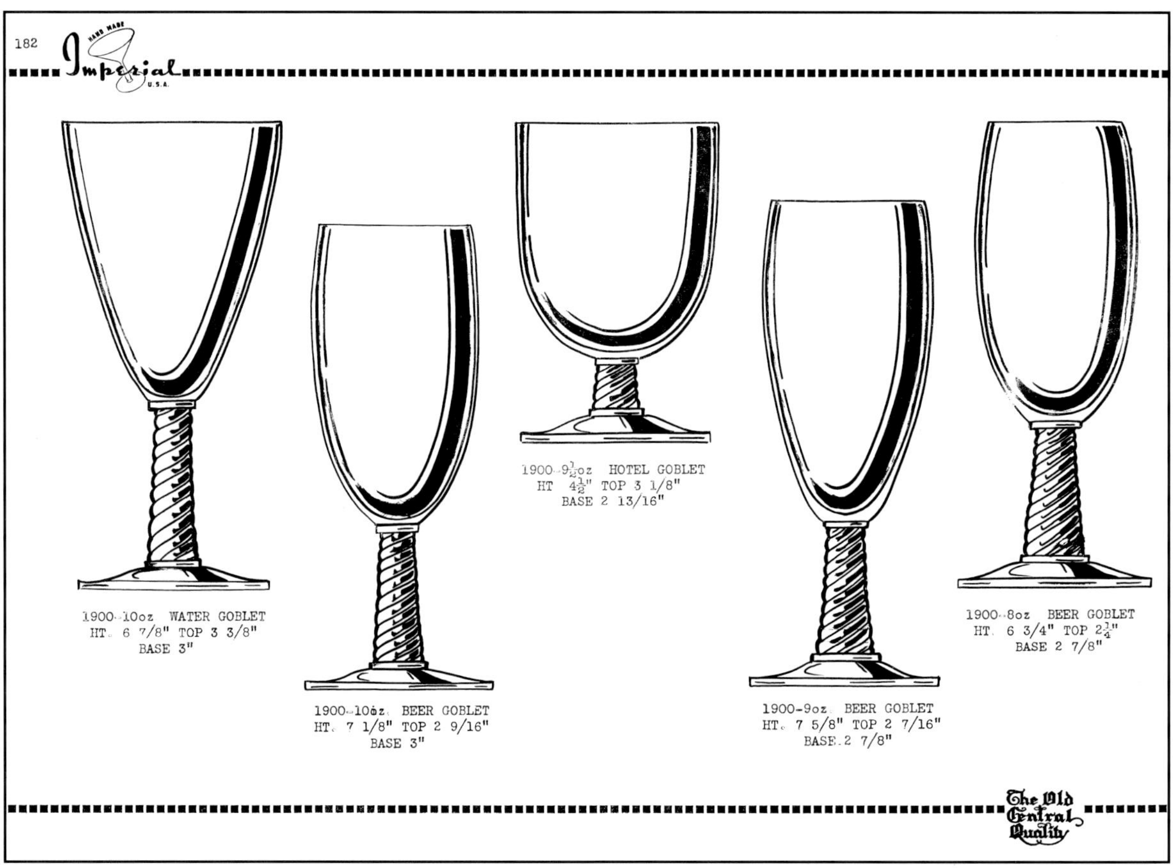


Catalog copy from 1939 Winslow #1900 line. *Author's Catalog.*

# #2000 Line

### Colors: rose, green, amber, orchid tints, crystal, and gold treated (black may be found)

The 2000 line is very small, consisting of compote or bonbon, candlesticks, and a few different rolled and straight edge bowls. The items most often found and recognized as being different from other manufacturers are the low candlesticks. These sticks are what I call the dual disk or dual separator line. In the area between the foot and the candleholder body you will find two round discs in the stem. Most of the other manufacturers did not use any separator or used just the one. Central is the only manufacturer to have made this design. The real confusion in the 2000 line is when dealing with the similarities between manufacturers of the mayonnaise/whipped cream servers, console bowls, and compotes. Everyone made the mayonnaise dish like the one shown here in the catalog reprints. One way to tell the Central item if the piece is not etched is to have the original spoon. The handle of the spoon starts at the bottom of the side of the bowl, pulls or arches up, then bends back down finally bending 90 degrees. Some even curl slightly back towards the bowl at the end of the handle. Tiffin and Fenton spoons are more similar in shape but the handle stem starts from the middle or higher up the side of the bowl. Cambridge spoons do not share the handle arch design. Also know your colors to further determine spoon makers, and watch for spoons by other companies when the originals have been lost or broken.

The best way to tell a Central mayo/whipped cream is the under plate. As in the cracker trays, the plate curves upward on much more of an incline than Cambridge or Tiffin lines, almost like a shallow dinner soup bowl. And, the indent that holds the foot of the bowl (which will be either rayed in the center or not) is perched or raised higher than similar products. In the body of the dish there are no real differences and company colors are the best indicator of manufacturer.

Compotes between Tiffin and Central are always confused, so the catalog reprints and images should give a better understanding of just who made what. Remember to read the article on Central/Tiffin and the Combines at the rear of this reference book.

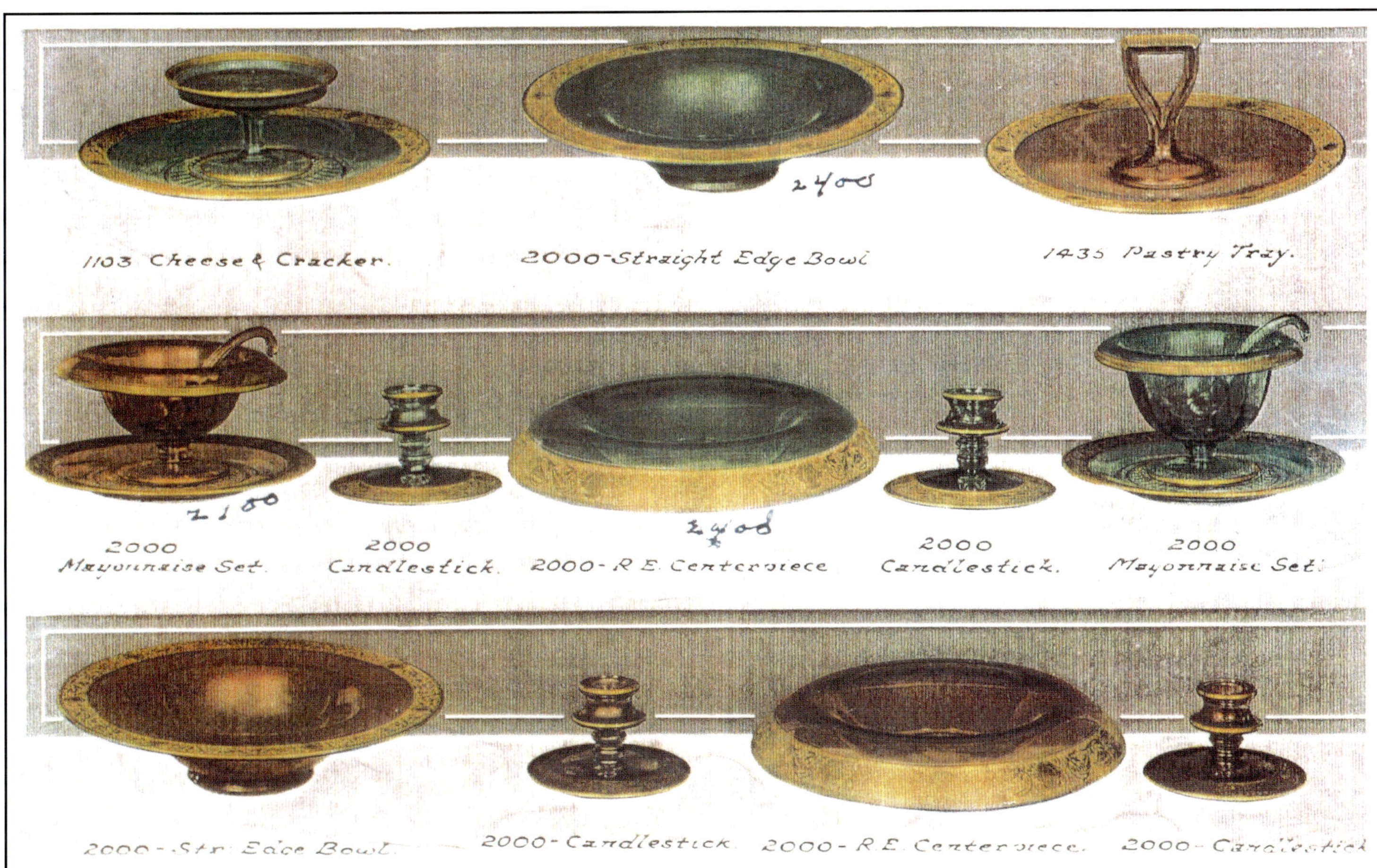


#2000 line. *Catalog Copy Courtesy Dean Six.*

#2000 line mayo and liner, amber, $45-$60 with correct spoon.

**Below:**
#2000 liner plate for mayo showing raised lip of indent and deep angle of plate, $10.

**Below:**
#2000 compote or bon-bon in rose color, 5-1/16" tall, $50.

#2000 dual disc candle in amber, $35.

# #2001 Line

### Colors: green, rose, amber, orchid tints, and crystal combinations

This line will also be just serving pieces or accessories for the table. Mayonnaise or whipped-creams, bowls, vases, salt & pepper, cigarette box, fruit basket, and trays make up the line. As I had written for the 2000 line, the mayo/whipped-creams are the same in both the 2000 and 2001 lines, and the descriptions on those items will be found in the 2000 section. The 8-inch flip vase will be found with a plain, paneled or drape/festoon optic. This causes a bit of concern for collectors trying to find out which company made their vase. The festoon or drape optic is easy to distinguish between Central and an almost identical Fostoria product. In the Fostoria vases the drape effect continues down the side and underneath the flat side of the vase and looks to gather towards the center. The 8-inch Central festoon/drape effect ends at the bottom of the vase and does not continue to the underside of the foot or flat area. In the paneled optic, or the plain versions, the best ways to tell these are Central products are by how thick the glass is at the bottom of the vase and by color. Central vases do not have as much glass gathered at the bottom as Fostoria vases do. And again, colors are important.

The fruit basket and muffin trays are a design all their own that should not be easy to confuse with anybody else's. While the handles are often confused with Imperial's, the bodies of the bowl area are easy to identify as Central's. The cigarette holder or box, as they call it in the sales brochure, should put an end to them all being attributed to other companies.

#2001 line pitcher and tumblers. *Author's Catalog.*

2001 handled basket, etched Veninga, $125.

#2001 8" flip vase in rose color, $40-50.

# #2002 Line

## Colors: green, rose, amber, & decorated and/or trimmed with gold

This line is also small with a bell bowl, cake plate, and four-footed salver. These pieces are always confused with Imperial due to the fact that nobody has ever seen the catalog images to try to tell the two manufacturers' products apart. Use the catalog images to verify the Central handles on the bowls and cake plate. The salver has four feet, and the glass is very heavy and thick. Although not pictured in the catalog, I'm sure the big rectangular bowl and liner plate belong to this line.

2002 line *Catalog Copy Courtesy Dean Six.*

#2002 oval serving bowl, 12" handle to handle, and platter, 15-1/2", amber, $60-80.

#2002 serving bowl, rose, 15-1/2", $60-75.

#2002 whip cream dish crystal, no etching, $12-15.

# #2005 Line

### Colors: rose, green, amber, orchid tints, and crystal, also gold encrusted

The 2005 line is slightly larger than most of the table service lines we have discussed earlier. Pieces that finally get their place in history are the cream soup & liner plate, the grapefruit & liner plate, the baked apple bowl, cup and saucer, candy box/covered relish with fleur-de-lis style finial, as well as the lily (low rolled edge console) bowl, 12-inch meat platter, grill plate, and the 7-inch compote.

While the mentioned pieces getting their historical attribute is overdue, some comments are necessary to stop a flood of responses by observant readers of this reference. The sales flyer copy shows the 2005 – 7-inch compote, improperly listed as a "2007"-7-inch comport. This piece belongs here with the 2005 items, as found in many other catalogs. It is just a misprint in the 1928 flyer. Yes, the 12-inch meat platter looks like Cambridge Glass Company's meat platter in their "Round Line" of dinnerware; it is identical from the scalloped handles to the rayed design in the center of the platter. The cream soup was given a second duty in life. While the piece was still hot enough to work with, a worker would have pulled the sides outward and down towards the base, making it a candy or lemon dish. While some reference pages by Central will call the round covered dish a covered relish, other references call it a three part covered candy. Call it what you will, and fill it with what you want, the name for this piece is, "Baker's Candy Box".

A quick word about saucer and liner plates, I believe is necessary to avoid confusion. The saucer measures almost 5-3/4-inches across by 11/16-inches tall. The saucer also has a perched or raised cup ring and is shaped almost like a bowl. The cream soup liner measures 6-1/4-inches across by 7/8-inches tall and has no raised ring for the soup bowl but is deep shaped just like the saucer. Bread and butter plates by Central are flat and measure the same 6-1/4-inches across as the soup liner.

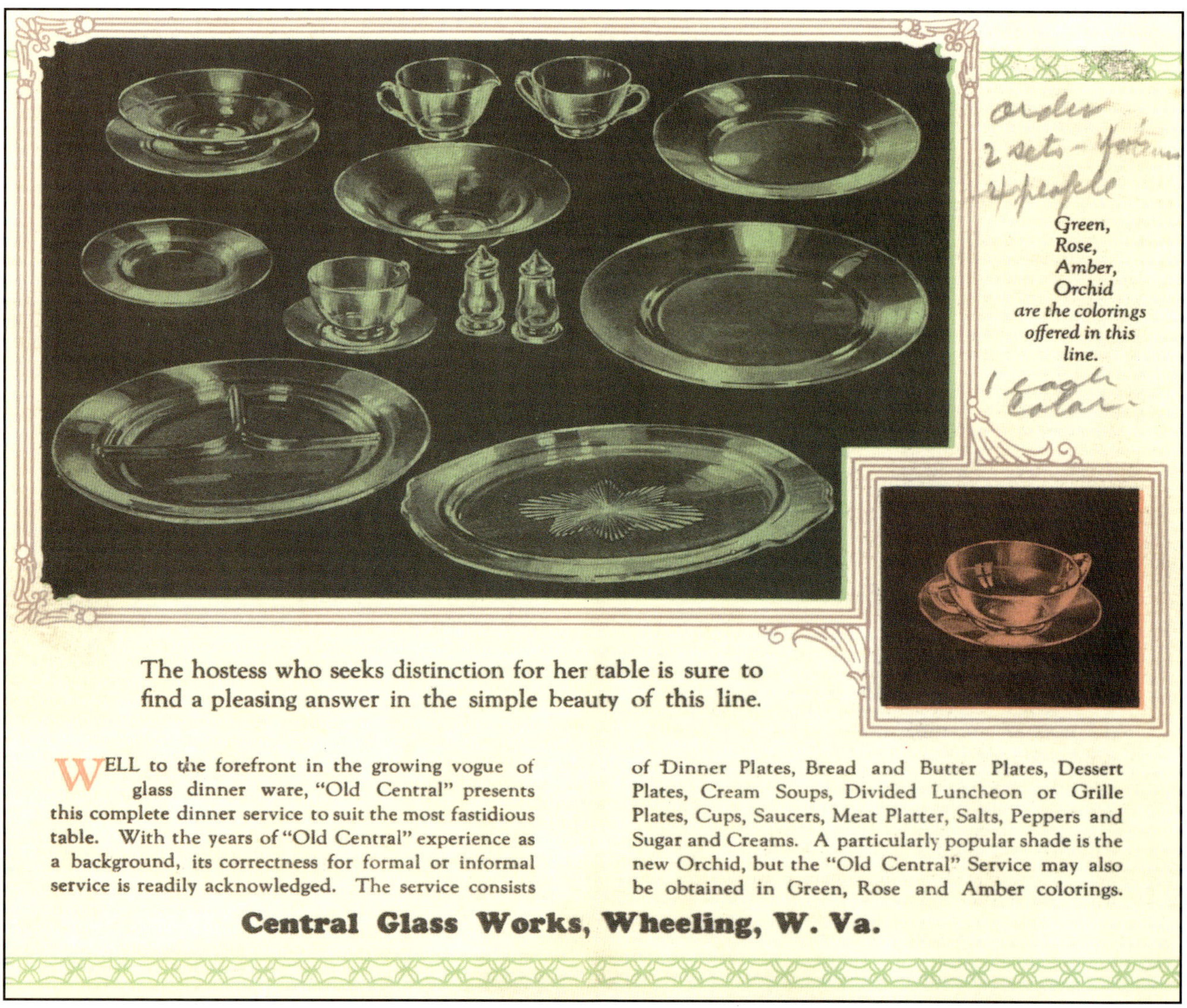


2005 line catalog copy. *Author's Catalog.*

DINNER LINE

SHOWN above are recent additions to the famous "Old Central" Dinner Line. Included are the No. 2005 Grille Plate, No. 2005 12 inch Meat Platter, No. 2005 Cream Soup and Plate, No. 1384½ Salad Plate, No. 2005 Grape Fruit and Plate, No. 2005 Cream and Sugar, No. 2005 Baked Apple, No. 2005 Cup and Saucer and No. 2001 Salt and Pepper.

3

2005 line catalog copy. *Author's Catalog.*

#2005 comport, 6" tall, 7" across top, $20-25.

#2005 cream soup and liner plate, amber, $25-30.

#2005 two handled bon-bon, $15-18.

#2005 footed bon-bon, 5-3/8" wide, 3-3/8" tall, rose, $30-40.

#2005 cup & saucer, crystal, $18-20.

#2005 12" meat platter, rose color, $18-20.

#2005 crystal covered candy *Baker's Candy Box*, $30-50.

# #2007 Line

### Colors: amber, green, rose, blue, and colors with crystal

While the trade journal copy of the 2007 line is kind of weak, I had the kids (when they were younger) color it up some to see if we could make the picture a wee bit better. And what a great job they've done, right? Still, the image is a little fuzzy, however this looks like the four graduated bead stem line that keeps popping up everywhere or will be known as the more common stem line produced by CGW. The beads start small and get larger (just as in the #1462 line) as they move up the stem towards the bowl. The colors listed by the company, just amber and green, do not fit. I have seen both solid amber and green stems in this line but more often the stems are found in combinations of colors and crystal, and rarely in blue and crystal. Unless I have this stem line confused with another due to image quality of the *Trade Journal* report, it's the only reference I have for it, so for now we'll stick with this story. The greatest thing about your attempt at research is, if you are wrong, you *will* be corrected. Thus, the learning continues.

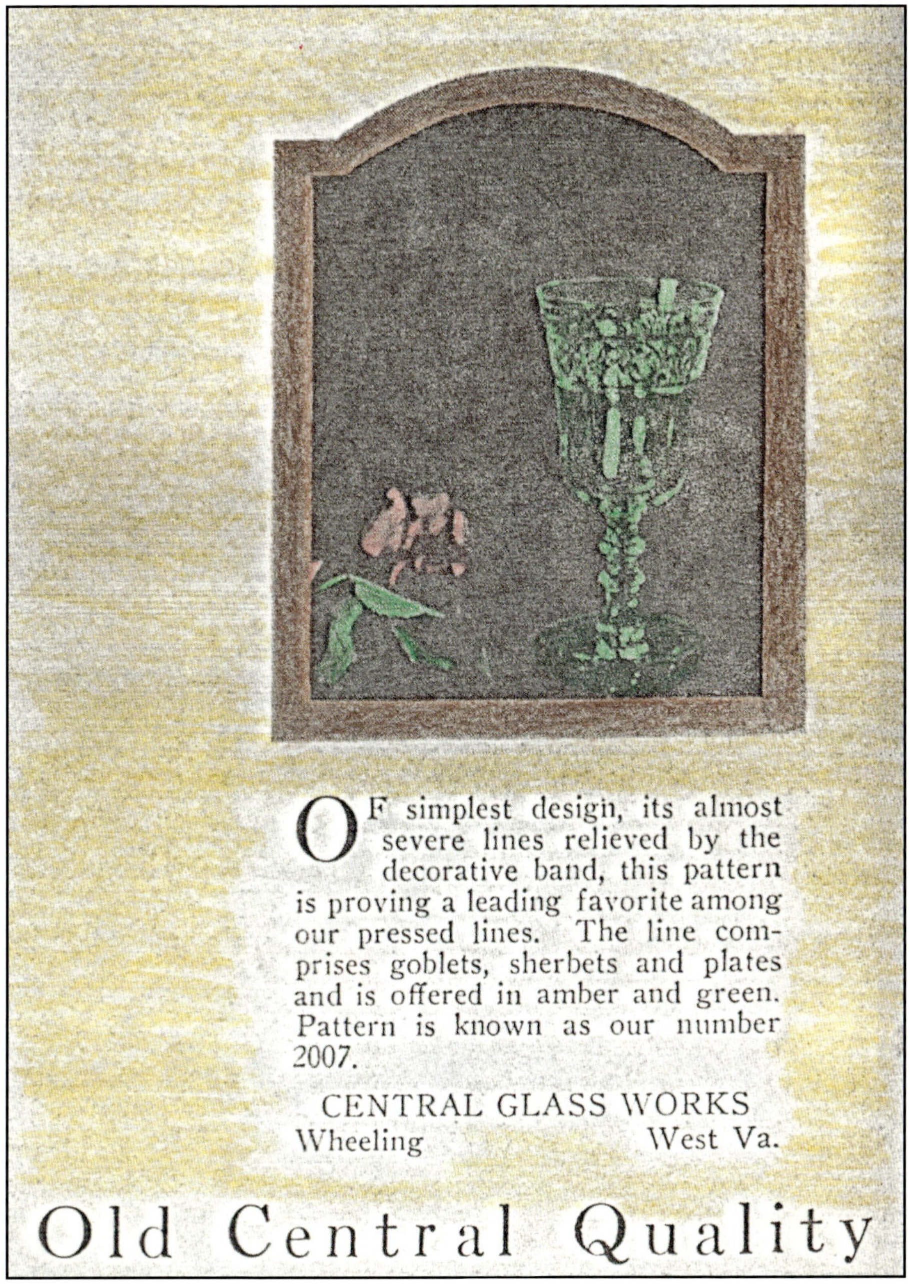
OF simplest design, its almost severe lines relieved by the decorative band, this pattern is proving a leading favorite among our pressed lines. The line comprises goblets, sherbets and plates and is offered in amber and green. Pattern is known as our number 2007.

CENTRAL GLASS WORKS
Wheeling West Va.

Old Central Quality

Small trade journal reprint #2007 stem line.

#2007 stem line, beads graduate from bottom, blue/crystal (without etch).

# #2010 Line Frances

### Colors: include rose, green, amber, orchid tints, light turquoise, blue, clambroth, and black. Also, satin finished black, crystal, green, and rose. Recently discovered: hand-painted items

The gorgeous 2010 line or Frances pattern has been found in all the great Central colors except Golden Sapphire so far. This Central line is very well made of the best metals and materials and is quite heavy for the time period making it one of the strongest of the Central patterns. Pieces in this pattern are being discovered today that amaze me. Satin finished candy jars of different sizes, with different style knobs and ashtrays, have surfaced. Pitchers, tumblers, goblets, and accessory items are very rare and hard to find without damage. And, while the three-footed bowls can be found in pink, green, and amber as the most common items, pieces such as candy boxes in any color and items in black, blue, and orchid tints should be grabbed without hesitation. The green handled nappy has never been seen before and must have been a special order item made by flattening a one handled nappy bowl while still hot. It wasn't inexpensive when I bought it, but I had never seen one like it.

The vases were shaped by holding the marie (the ring on the base of a piece of glass) and, while still in a very hot state from the oven, swinging to create different lengths. The more the glass craftsman would swing, the longer the piece would be. The finisher would then use wooden tools to shape the top area of the vase. Because of this, there will be no two vases produced that will be the same. This will also be true of the three-footed bowls and servers. They did not however get the swinging treatment, but were hand-formed while hot. Also, the big low console bowl in Frances started its life out of the mold as a vase. While still in a state where it could be shaped, it was merely pushed down to form the rolled out look of a console bowl.

This line's roots can be traced back to the Chippendale line earlier in the company's history.

Special thanks go out to Roni Sionakides for her early and continuing contributions in the research of this pattern. Also, to Rick Hirte & Susie Thompson, for bringing to light the name for the ashtray, hence forth to be known as "Uncle Bucky's Ashtray".

The snuffer lid has two tapered holes for snuffing out your cigarette, two horizontal sets of rests to hold the smoke while not needed, and one larger hole in the center to dispose of the cigarette when finished. In the Uncle Bucky folklore, one would fill the ashtray with sand to further extinguish the cigarette when finished.

| Item | size | crystal | rose/ green | amber | black/ orchid/ blue |
|---|---|---|---|---|---|
| Ash tray | | | $125 | | $125/175/ 125 |
| Bowl berry | | | $155 | $45-50 | |
| Bowl master berry | | | $85-95 | $85 | |
| Bowl 3 ftd. | various shapes | $25 | $40-55 | $30-45 | |
| Bowl console | marie base | $30 | $50-65 | $40-50 | |
| Bowl trophy | footed/ handled | | $65 | $55 | |
| Candle sticks | | | $75-95 | | |
| Candy dish | | $35 | $75-95 | $50-65 | $95/125/ 140 |
| Comport | footed w/ handles | $75 | $75-90 | | |
| Comport | low no handles | $35 | | | |
| Creamer | footed | $30 | $50-65 | $50-65 | |
| Nappy handled | | | $225 | | |
| Pitcher ftd. | | | $175-225 | $125-150 | |
| Plate | 6-in. | $12 | $18-22 | $18-22 | |
| Plate | 11-in. | $18 | $25-40 | $20-25 | |
| Server | Center handle | $45 | $65-80 | $45.00-50 | |
| Server | 3 ftd. | $25 | $35-50 | $35-45 | |
| Stem | goblet/ spooner | $25 | $55-75 | $45-50 | |
| Sugar | footed | $30 | $50-65 | $50-65 | |
| Tumbler | flat | $75-100 | $75-100 | | |
| Vase Tall | varies in ht. | $55-70 | $95-125 | $65-75 | $125/150/ 150 |

#2010 line Frances-crystal tall vase, $55-70.

#2010 line Frances trade journal reprint C. 1929.

#2010 line Frances-black tall vase, $125-150.

#2010 line Frances *Uncle Bucky's Ash Tray*, rose, $125-150.

#2010 line Frances-*Uncle Bucky's Ash Trays*, green and black (no cover shown), $125-150 complete.

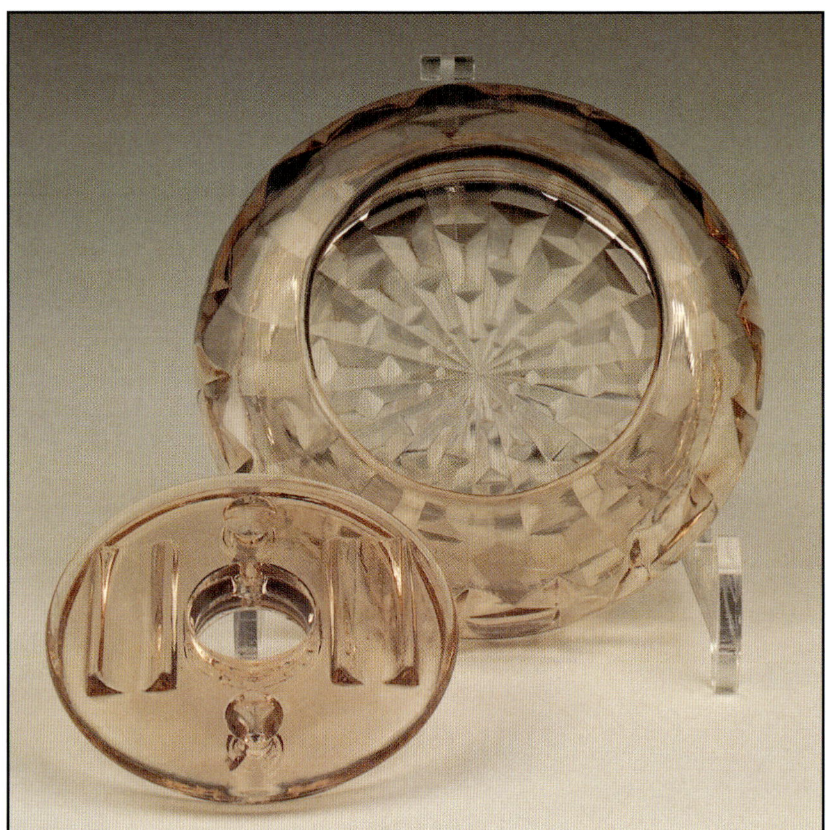

#2010 line Frances-ash tray cover/ snuffer showing inside pattern in bottom.

#2010 line Frances-water pitcher, rose, $175-225.

#2010 line Frances-candle holder, 3-1/2" tall, rose, $45 each.

#2010 line Frances-covered candy, satin finished green, $50-60.

#2010 line Frances-small berry bowl, 4-1/4" across, 2" tall, rose color, $135-160.

#2010 line Frances-one handled flattened nappy, green, 7" handle to end, $225.

#2010 line Frances-creamer and sugar, green color, $130-140.

#2010 line Frances-creamer and sugar, rose color, $125-130.

#2010 line Frances - flat tumbler, rose, 10 oz., 4-1/8" tall, $75-100.

#2010 line Frances-master berry set, amber 8" master and 6" small berry, $350-375.

**Right:**
#2010 line Frances-crystal low footed compote, 5-1/4" tall, $35.

**Center:**
#2010 line Frances-green 3 footed bowl, 9-7/8" across, 4-1/8" tall, $40-55.

**Bottom:**
#2010 line Frances-rose colored 3 footed server, 11-3/4" across, 2-3/8" tall, $35-50.

#2010 line Frances-3 footed bowl, 2 areas pulled down, in rose color, $40-55.

#2010 line Frances-green 3 footed server, 11-3/4" across, 2-3/8" tall, $35-50.

#2010 line Frances-3 footed bowl, 3 areas pulled down, in amber color, $30-45.

#2010 line Frances-large console bowl,12-3/4" across, formed from a vase while still in a molten state, amber, $40-50.

#2010 line Frances-large console bowl,12-3/4" across, formed from a vase while still in a molten state, amber, view from lower area, $40-50.

**Below:**
#2010 line Frances-large console bowl,12-3/4" across, formed from a vase while still in an almost molten state, green, $50-65.

#2010 line Frances-3 footed bowl with rolled edge in rose color,$35-50.

#2010 line Frances tall vase in amber, $65-75.

#2010 line Frances tall vase in rose color, $95-125.

#2010 line Frances tall vases in green, showing the different height, and tooling performed while pieces were still very hot, $95-125 each.

#2010 line Frances 3 footed bowl pulled down in 3 areas, in rose color, $40-55.

#2010 line Frances-green footed trophy bowl, partial satin finish, 11-1/2" across handle to handle, 6-3/16" tall to top of handle, $45-50.

# #2014 Line

## Console Bowl: Crystal, Colors, and Decorated

The only item I have in this line is a six-toed or footed console bowl. Hopefully, more items will be added as more information becomes available. Adding this blank as being a CGW product, though, is historically important. There is an image of the bowl on the catalog copy with the lower right corner missing.

#2014 six toed console bowl, crystal, $15-18; colors, $20-25.

#2014 six toed console bowl, view of foot area.

# #2019 Line

### Colors: amber, green, rose, crystal, black, and Golden Sapphire

Here finally is proof that these pieces are not Cambridge. For years these blanks have been sold as part of Cambridge's famous "Key Hole Line." While very similar in the handles, there are differences that the close-ups (Look-A-Likes Section) will show.

The important thing to remember on the Central line is, on Central's 2019 you could easily get two fingers through the handle. In fact it looks as though you could also use it as a bottle opener.

How many pieces there actually are in the line will be up to you to discover. The catalog shot (find catalog copy in the section covering the 2025 console bowl) shows just a couple of small lemon or bon-bon plates. They will be found flat or with turned up sides. I'm sure we will discover mayonnaise and whipped cream dishes as well as other sizes of bowls with this scalloped design and keyhole style open handles. Also, this pattern is shown in New Martinsville catalogs as the 2019 line and is identical to Central's. Don't forget to stop by the Look-A-Likes section for more on this.

| Item | amber/rose/green | black |
|---|---|---|
| Lemon plate | $15-22 | $25 |
| Candy, up-turned handles | $18-22 | $25 |
| Preserve | $22-25 | $25 |

#2019 bon-bon or candy, ebony, $25.

#2019 bon-bon or candy, Golden Sapphire, $25.

# #2020 Line

### Crystal, rose, amber, green, black, and decorated

This 2020 is the line number appointed to this deco looking candle that was sold with the 2025 line of bowls. (See catalog copy of the 2025 bowl.) So far I have been unable to buy one for an example. Deco collectors must be more excited about their finds than glass collectors. More often than not they are listed as being made by Fry. They sell for $75-100 each with no decoration

# #2025 Line

### Colors: amber, rose, green, black (so far!)

This deco style of bowls is just coming to the surface as being Central. For years it was being attributed to other companies, most often referred to as New Martinsville. The bowls are found in many different shapes, having been tooled by craftsman depending on the customer's specific needs, even fish bowls. There are also different sizes of bowls hinting that smaller and larger blanks were used and not just one mold. The base of the blank is usually the same size on all the bowls, the only difference being the upper body area.

Also important to note is that the bottom of the base should not contact the item it is sitting on, such as a table. The three feet on the bottom of the base are tall enough that there will not be base contact. I have seen bowls that the feet have been ground down flat on, and that is not the way they were produced. Look in this area for damage or repair.

The catalog copy showing this bowl is a very exciting page. Not only is the deco bowl shown but also the 2020 line candle as well as many other long unknown blanks and etching examples.

| Item | size | amber/rose/green | black |
|---|---|---|---|
| Bowl fruit | 10-1/2 | $45-60 | $65 |
| Bowl fruit | 12" | $55-70 | $95 |
| Bowl Fish | ball shape | $85-95 | |

#2025 deco bowl line as well as other lines *Catalog Copy Courtesy Dean Six* .

#2025 line bowl, black,12" across top, 5-1/2" tall, $95.

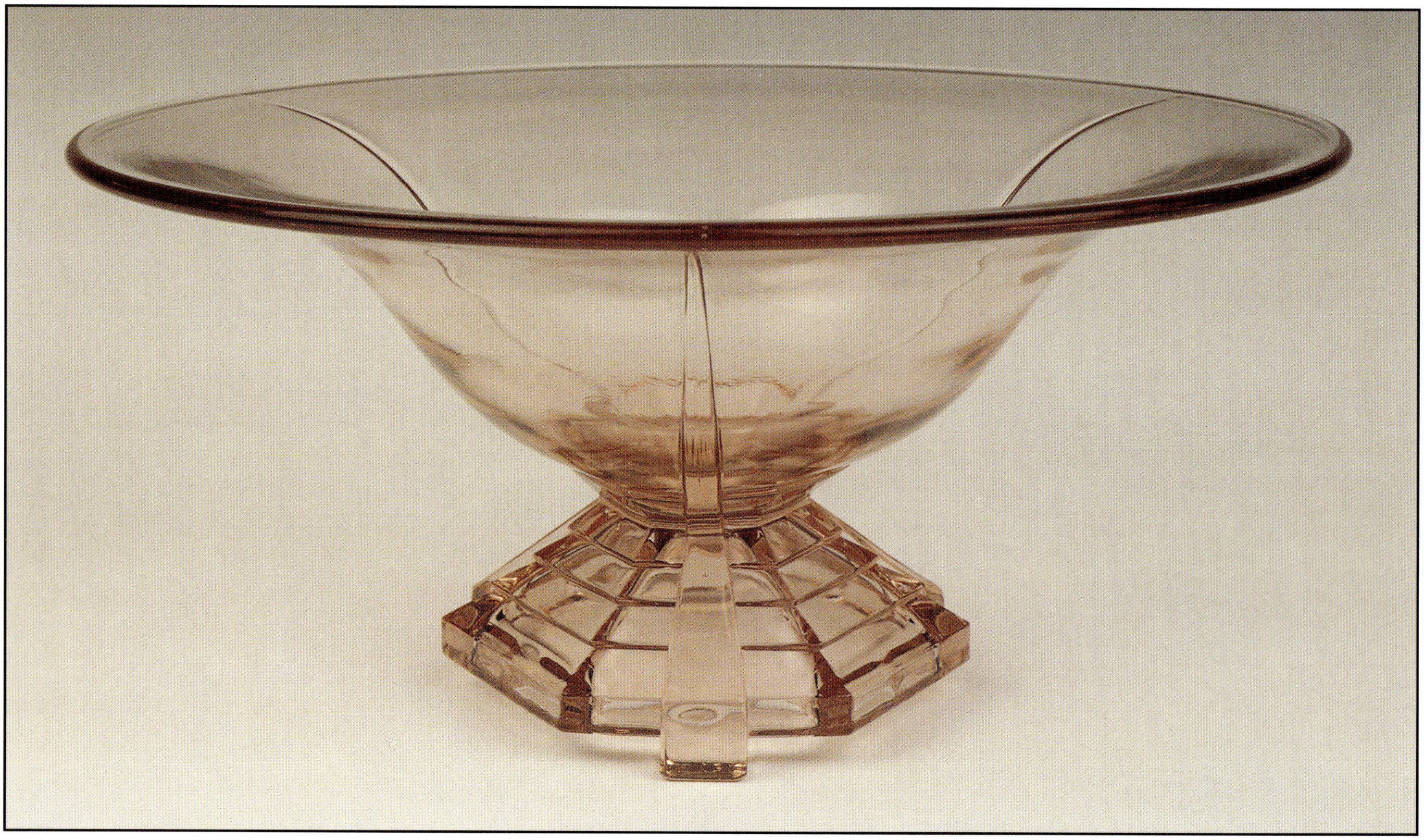

#2025 line bowl, rose color, 10-1/4" across top, 5" tall, $40-60.

# Miscellaneous Lines / Unknown Lines

## Crystal, Colors, and Combinations

The following examples will be of miscellaneous lines where you will find these wares etched by Central Glass Works. Keep in mind there are hundreds of other lines by this company, but I thought showing those line numbers most often used in home table services would be better and take less room in this reference, than giving all the lines (also I have not found them all yet) produced. This is meant to give you a quick reference when you find an etched example, or possibly a blank you haven't been able to identify.

#68 Ale 6-1/2 oz., looks like a flared vase with a ball stem just above the foot

#117 Tumblers are the hour glass shape (see catalog copy)

#301 Tumblers from 3-14 ounces are found (see photo)

#364 Goblet can be seen in the trade journal copy along with #720 & #815 goblets

#403 or "Touraine" is the factory name for this line of tumblers. The line will have examples measuring from 3-14 ounces (see catalog copy)

#530 or "St. Regis" is actually Central's factory name for this line of tumblers (see photo)

#530 Finger bowl blown, 14 oz. (copy)

#731 Handled Ice Tea, 11 oz.

#733 Tea Pot with cover, ball finial. Although catalogs show this item, I have never seen one (see ad copy). This item may have been extremely fragile, and did not hold up during or after production

#800 Finger bowl, very fragile and light.

#818 Goblet, pulled stem, is available in a complete line. Made in plain, diamond or paneled optic.

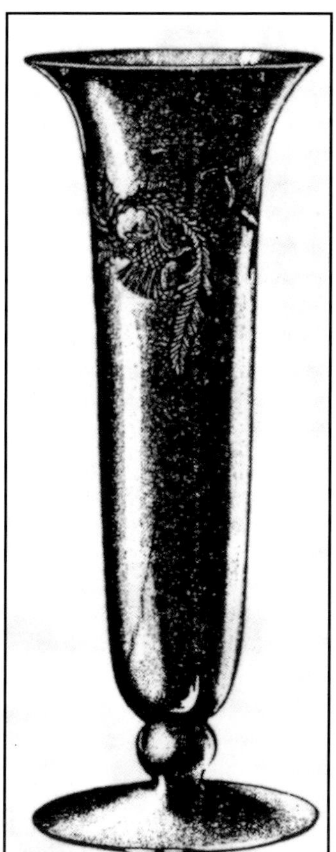

#68 Ale glass holds 6-1/2 oz.

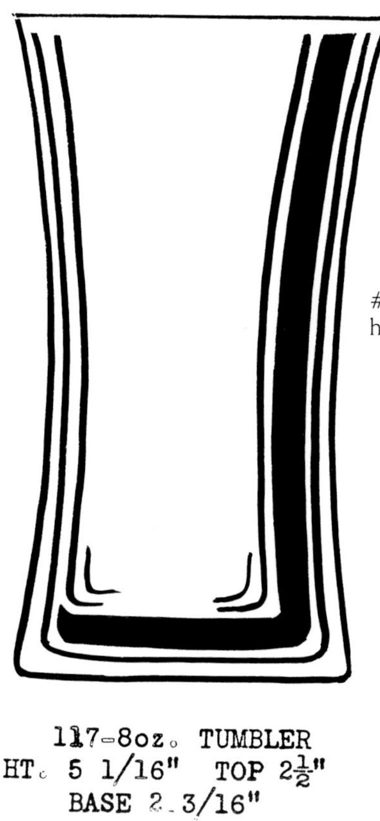


#117 line of tumblers, hour glass shape.

#301 table tumbler, #530 or St. Regis table tumbler, and #1096 table tumbler, $5-6 each.

Trade journal copy showing goblets #364, #720, and #815 from 1917.

#403 Touraine line,12 oz. table tumbler shown.

#530 St. Regis finger bowl, without etch $8-10.

#731 handled ice tea, 11 oz., 5-1/4" tall, $12-15 without etch.

#733 teapot, unable to price due to scarcity, best guess would be $500-600.

#800 finger bowl, top and bottom view. $6-8 without an etch.

#818 goblet with diamond optic, 7-1/4" tall, 9 oz., rose color, $15-20.

## Table Tumblers

### Crystal, but some colors may be found

Just a few short words about table tumblers by Central. The biggest and most often seen line of tumblers is the 530 or St. Regis line. In this line the tumbler is rather straight up the sides from the bottom until you reach the top ten percent, at which point it flares outward. More often than not the blank is paneled or has an optic (vertical lines). The St. Regis was made in sizes from 2-1/2 oz. to, according to the catalog, a 14 oz. size, but I have uncovered 16 oz. examples. The 16 oz. St. Regis tumbler measures 5-5/8-inches tall. The 1096 table tumbler seems to have been the only one made in this line and is much more sturdy than the 530 product. The 1096 measures 3-3/4-inches tall and holds 9 oz. This tumbler has no flared lip, but may be found with special cuts along the lower bottom area. Different width and/or height cuts were given different cut numbers such as "Cut 7". A cut would resemble someone taking a spoon and scraping down the bottom outside of the tumbler in uniform fashion, all the way around the tumbler or similar piece of glass.

The 301 tumbler looks like the 530 in that it flares out, but the flare starts farther down the side of the blank, just about half way up the side. These should be found in all the same sizes as the St Regis (530) line.

## Dresser/Vanity Tray

### Colors: rose, green, and amber; may be found in ebony

This is the dresser or vanity tray by Central Glass Works. Although the only example I have has the celluloid cover, it will also be found with a glass cover and a finial knob that more matches the drawing issued by the Patent Office.

| Item | cover | rose/ green | amber | ebony |
|---|---|---|---|---|
| Vanity Tray | celluloid cover | $125 | $110 | |
| Vanity Tray | glass cover | $175 | $150 | |

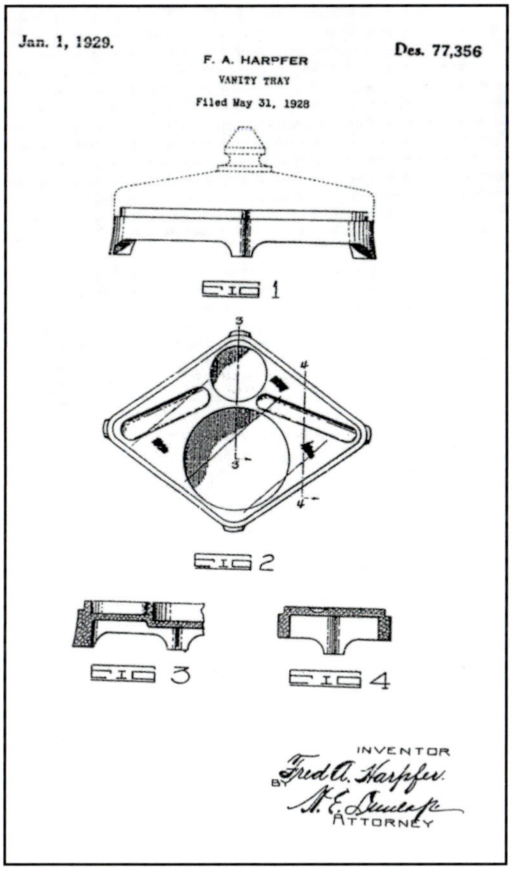


Vanity tray, patent office copy.
*Courtesy of Helen & Bob Jones.*

**Patented Jan. 1, 1929.** **Des. 77,356**

**UNITED STATES PATENT OFFICE.**

**FRED A. HARPFER, OF WHEELING, WEST VIRGINIA, ASSIGNOR TO CENTRAL GLASS WORKS, OF WHEELING, WEST VIRGINIA, A CORPORATION OF WEST VIRGINIA.**

**DESIGN FOR A VANITY TRAY.**

**Application filed May 31, 1928. Serial No. 26 940. Term of patent 3½ years.**

*To all whom it may concern:*

Be it known that I, FRED A. HARPFER, a citizen of the United States of America, and resident of Wheeling, county of Ohio, and State of West Virginia, have invented a new, original, and ornamental Design for a Vanity Tray, of which the following is a specification, reference being had to the accompanying drawings, in which—

Fig. 1 is a side elevation of a vanity tray, showing my new design;

Fig. 2 is a top plan view of the same; and—

Figs. 3 and 4 are sections taken, respectively, on lines 3—3 and 4—4, Fig. 2.

I claim—

The ornamental design for a vanity tray, as shown.

FRED A. HARPFER.

Vanity tray with celluloid cover in rose, $125.

Vanity tray with celluloid cover in rose, inside view, $125.

# Chippendale Pattern or Krys-Tol

## Crystal only by Central Glass Works

Chippendale is the name for the colonial line that originated with the Ohio Flint Glass Company. It was heavily produced not only for customers here in the States, but was distributed heavily in the United Kingdom as well as Australia. In 1908 the Ohio Flint Glass Company sold the patents and molds to the Jefferson Glass Company of West Virginia, who in 1919 sold it to Central Glass Works.

Central's "largest" market was barware at that time, and with the country going dry due to Prohibition, they found themselves in need of different lines of wares if they were to stay in business. Acquisition of the Chippendale pattern would fill the void left by the absence of the barware market here in the states, and prove to take them beyond what they imagined possible to that point. When Central acquired the Krys-Tol patterns and molds, they also acquired the customer base that already enjoyed a large established market. The following is an excerpt from an article in the trade publication, *China Glass and Lamps*, dated April 28th, 1919:

> The loss in bar glassware as the result of the country going dry will not affect the Central Glass Works, of Wheeling, West Virginia, as much as was anticipated. The business turned over by the Jefferson Glass Company in Chippendale ware has been so great the company finds itself unable to fill all orders. The first improvements decided on by the directors will be in the factory, which will have to be rebuilt. This plant will be three stories in height and modern in every respect. The present selling force will be increased by the engaging of several European representatives. Charles J. Pratt, who has represented the Jefferson in London for many years, will continue to sell Chippendale and the present product of the Central in Great Britain. Mr. Pratt's foreign trade has been very large and the orders turned over by the Jefferson will run into huge sums. The demand in England for glassware is growing every day. The improvements planned will give employment to an additional 75 or 100 more people and when the new factory is started in full there will be three furnaces of 36 pots. After these improvements are completed, the Central will have one of the most modern and up-to-date glass plants in the country, manufacturing the highest grade of glassware turned out

Considering what we've seen in the obituary, where it would appear Central was a nothing company, here we find worldwide routes of business proving a strength and Central in command of market-share among the top dogs of the glass industry.

During a trip out west on vacation we happened to stop in an antique shop in Anacortes, Washington, when I had noticed some pieces of colonial pattern glass marked on the bottom Krys-Tol. While looking the pieces over, the clerk who had seen my interest stated that these pieces were fresh back from England, as the shop owner had just returned from a buying trip. I attempted to enlighten the clerk that the items were made in West Virginia and then shipped to England, and it would appear finally found their way back to the states. The clerk made several attempts to correct me and straighten me out to the fact that these pieces of Krys-Tol had to be made in England. Who knows, perhaps she's right. Central did finally sell off the Chippendale line to a British firm named Davidson in 1933. So, maybe these pieces were in fact not ones that were made between the 1890s and 1933 in the West Virginia and Ohio area, but were in fact made by Davidson. And I'm not sure if Davidson kept the trademark name or not. There's more research necessary to unravel the history of the Chippendale pattern and the British connection.

The most commonly found pieces of Krys-Tol are the number T319-candlestick in the larger size and the T314 child's size. Keep in mind Heisey also made a similar candlestick in the child's size, so look closely for the Krys-Tol trademark on each piece. The other piece that seemed to be very popular is the number T76 two handled comport. I have seen examples of this piece that were very large, almost resembling a centerpiece. If I recall correctly, it must have been 15-inches tall and 12-inches across, and it was a spectacular old lead crystal example. Most examples you will see will be the average size of 9-inches tall. Something else worth noting is that Westmoreland did somehow acquire the mold for this two handled comport, and produced examples in colors during the 1950s and 1960s. These are still found occasionally with the original Westmoreland stickers still attached. Also found in these colors are creamers and sugars and covered butter dishes.

The Chippendale pattern was advertised to and purchased by America's First Families, those who would have higher end American made crystal products in their homes. The pattern was also very durable and used heavily by the hotel industry.

The trademark names are shown in the close-ups. Keep in mind when you are looking for that trademark that pieces produced from fresh made molds will have strong or easy to read markings, and pieces that came from molds that have been heavily used will show weaker examples of the trademark logo. In the large stick, the name is clearly legible on the bottom of the center shaft near the base and requires no cross-eyed stand on your head stare to read it. On the little child's stick, on the other hand, it is very hard to locate that trademark as it runs from the bottom just above the base, up toward the middle. On the little Toy, Child's, or Jack Be Nimble candleholder, it is found on top of the base running horizontal above the foot.

The space needed to list and discuss the Chippendale pattern would fill a book all by itself, so there will only be these few examples to show. This is a very large line with covered jugs with covers that lock in place to keep them from toppling into the beverages. Other pieces found will be refrigerator jugs, punch bowls, tumblers of many sizes and shapes, decanters, goblets, creamers and sugars of all sizes, compotes (footed, flared, and not), crushed fruit and candy jars with covers, bowls of all sizes and styles, cruets, vases, trays of all sizes, and even a Georgian style design. Also, it would be interesting to note that this is probably the only general line produced by Central in which a handled basket will be found.

Many of the blanks CGW used in the coming years were carry-overs of this popular line: the 1419 jug and the 1103 server just to name a couple. Also, this is where the Frances or 2010 line will have found its roots. Once you take a look at the Chippendale, you can see how the 2010 line evolved from there.

Chippendale 4-1/2" child's candlestick, $45.

Chippendale 9" candlestick with cuttings (shown with child's size candle for comparison) in mint condition, $55-75.

Chippendale Toy, Child's, or Jack Be Nimble candlestick, $45-60 each.

Chippendale individual celery salt dip, $22-25.

Columbian Coin tall covered sugar, $395-425.

## Columbian Coin

### Crystal only

The coin pattern is another line that will be earlier in Central's history and I would recommend the Schiffer Publication by author Marilyn Hallock titled *Central Glass The First Thirty Years*. Shown here will be the tall covered sugar and the toothpick. The Coin pattern has been written about in several books and therefore not a pattern that is unknown. The coins on this pattern were so well defined, the government ordered an immediate production stop on this line, allowed all stock to that point to be sold, then destroyed all of the molds.

Please be aware of reproductions. If you would collect this historical pattern, you will need to be informed as how to tell the legitimate pieces from fakes. There are many!

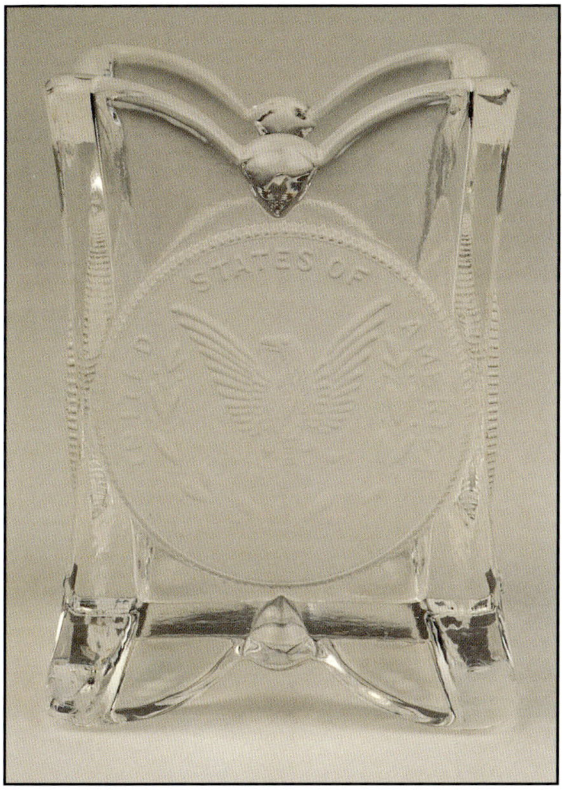

Columbian Coin toothpick holder, $175-210.

# Unknown Lines

### Known to be Central Glass Works Products

I thought it necessary to have an area for the "unknowns" we know to be CGW products but can't place with a line number. The discovery of the items to be Central products will come from trade journals or other sources leading us to be 100% positive (or almost certain anyway … well maybe just a strong hunch).

# Deco Fan

### Crystal, cobalt, as well as other colors should be found

The first line I wish to discuss I was always uncertain about Central ever having produced, until I happened across a creamer and sugar in crystal with the Hester etching. This was the evidence I needed. Many pieces are found in this blank with some fantastic cobalt colors and gold treated edging. Creamers and sugars, divided relish dishes, as well as large bowls with liner plates have been found.

Later, Imperial reissued this blank with such cuttings as "Belmont Hills". Until we can get an actual line number or pattern name from any old CGW reference, we'll just call this the Deco-Fan blank.

Deco Fan candlesticks, 4-13/16" tall, 4-1/8" base diameter, pair crystal, $55-75.

Deco Fan sugar, crystal, $15-18.

## Pamela

### Bowls of rich colors with crystal stems, early 1937

Pamela is shown only to date, as far as I know, in trade journal press releases, with this line released in the spring of 1937 showing the full line of stems with colored bowls and crystal stems. The stem reminds me of a beehive with its three bulbous rings separating the bowl from the shaft of the stem. Interestingly enough, Lotus Decorating, who was Central's biggest customer of undecorated blanks, wasted no time in releasing these blanks with their latest creations, known as Royal and Royal Windsor, just a few months later.

RIGHT OUT OF THE KILN

Zircon, A. H. Heisey's indescribably lovely new color in stemware and flat pieces, is neither green nor blue, but a jewel-like tone which combines both. The Saturn bowls illustrated above are made in this new shade and crystal.

Bowl and candlesticks above from the new Pristine line at Cambridge Glass Co. Cutting on the bowl is the attractive Neo-Classic.

Line of stemware below from Central Glass Co., shown by Francis H. Ruhe. The bowls are in rich colors, and the graceful stem and foot in clear crystal.

Imported salad bowl and plate above from Koscherak Bros. comes in crystal, rose, blue, or amber. There are two different shapes, and either make fine $1 retailers.

Decorations on the attractive pieces above from Mississippi Glass Co. were done by Wheeling Decorating Co. They are good in black and white or gold on the glass. J. Walter Green has these in New York.

Imported decanters of fine cut crystal in a new square shape from Fisher Bruce & Co. are shown below. They have a twenty ounce capacity, and may be retailed for about $5.

30 CROCKERY AND GLASS JOURNAL for March, [illegible]

Pamela Line, *Crockery and Glass Journal's* "Right Out Of The Kiln," March 1937.

**right out of the**

# KILN

● Hors d'oeuvre dish and bowl, pictured at lower left, from Mississippi Glass Co. at Fisher, Bruce & Co. These retail for $2 and $2.50 respectively and come in amber, green, light blue, deep blue, and wine, as well as crystal.

● Vegetable Kingdom, a new pattern from Taylor, Smith & Taylor Co., done in Nature's own colors is introduced at the lower right. Just about every conceivable variety of vegetable is represented in realistic fashion on this ware.

● Royal Windsor as regal as its name, with wide gold band border and ornate gold vine decoration. Crystal goblet is Royal, also embellished with the rich gold border. Both are from Lotus Glass Co., shown at top left.

● Newest departure at Duncan & Miller, illustrated second from top, lovely blown vases in deep blue, amber, green, light blue and crystal. These come in eight, ten and twelve inch sizes—the latter to retail for $1.98.

30 CROCKERY AND GLASS JOURNAL for June, 193

Central's Pamela blank in *Crockery and Glass Journal's* section, "Right Out Of The Kiln," showing etching by Lotus in their Royal and Royal Windsor patterns, June 1937.

Pamela goblets, 10 oz. water, 8" tall, $25-30; 6 oz. champagne, 6-1/8" tall, $22-25; 3 oz. cocktail, 5-1/4" tall, $22-25.

# Dual Bead & Faceted Jewel

## Colors: unknown

Looking more like Fostoria and Seneca blanks, these two odd stems have eluded me to this point. While I have seen the etchings, the stems still remain elusive. While the trade journal ad is dated 1932, it causes me much concern as this is one of the years CGW was sidelined by the depression and did not see much production. Did they make them, or just send out possible, or "in planning work," press releases?

And, while I have been unable to produce the line numbers for these blanks, in order to remember these stems, it seems the names Dual Bead for the stem shown on the right in the trade journal ad by Central would fit, and Faceted Jewel for the stem on the left will work until correct numbers are found for these lines.

*December, 1931*

profit. J. L. Hudson Co. are intent upon pursuing this course, and feel that if unswervingly followed it is bound to bring successful operation. They are not only insistent that china and glassware departments can be operated profitably, but are going a step further and proving it.

Three Score Years of Achievement

*(Continued from page 78)*

regulated to a scientific degree that insures its perfection. Durability as well as beauty is one of the goals in the finished ware. Metallic glazes of exceptional brilliance, matt glazes of radiant depth, underglaze paintings with clearly defined lines, are typical of the Weller products.

The latest of the Weller line, Sydonia, is an outstanding example of originality in design and execution. Taking humble marsh plants as the inspiration and the model the potter has made bowls, jugs and vases of the broad, deeply-fluted leaves, from the tubular roots as conceived bud vases and candlesticks from the open blossom of the marsh flower has devised cornucopias. In grayish blue or in a light green this ware is equally delightful.

The Weller factories at the present time are engaged in full-time production. So reasonably priced has been all the ware that it has made an appeal to the present low-price market and while some other factories languish for business, Weller forges ahead. Maintaining quality, experimenting with new glazes and new clay mixtures, reaching for better designs, the Weller group has built up a business that warrants the support it is receiving from the retail trade.

Calendar of Coming Shows

Jan. 4-16.—National Chicago Lamp Show, Merchandise Mart. Chicago.
Jan. 4-16—Winter Furniture Market, American Furniture Mart, Chicago.
Jan. 11-21—Pittsburgh Pottery and Glass Exhibit, Pittsburgh, Pa.
Jan. 11-15—New York Lamp Show, Hotel New Yorker, New York.
Feb. 1-6—National Artwares Show, Hotel Stevens, Chicago.
Feb. 1-6—Chicago Gift Show, Merchandise Mart, Chicago.
Feb. 1-12—Eastern Manufacturers & Importers Exhibit, Palmer House, Chicago.
Feb. 15-19—National Artwares Show, Hotel Adelphia, Philadelphia.
Feb. 22-26—National Artwares Show, Hotel Pennsylvania, New York.
Feb. 22-26—New York Gift Show, Hotel New Yorker, New York.
Feb. 29-Mar. 4—Boston Gift Show, Associated Eastern Exhibitors, Hotel Statler, Boston.
Feb. 29-Mar. 5—National Artwares Show, Hotel Copley-Plaza, Boston.



*Tell our advertisers you saw it in* The Crockery and Glass Journal

Trade journal copy showing the two stem lines Faceted Jewel and Dual Bead, c. 1932.

# Unknown Line Number Vases

While we know these vases to be Central Glass Works products, to this point we have not located their line numbers, but feel it's very important to add them here.

Green tall cylinder vase, poppy etch, *Courtesy Larry Baker,* $60-75.

Amber vase, crimped top, similar to one found etched with Morgan etch, *Courtesy Larry Baker* $45-60.

Tall amber vase, *Courtesy Larry Baker* $75-90.

# Pitchers, Jugs, and Tankards

## Crystal and Colors

Instead of grouping the pitchers, jugs, and tankards in with their individual line numbers, I thought it better to add a section on these marvelous beauties, thus keeping them closer together for a quicker overall reference. There are many pitchers and jugs that I have the line numbers for, but no examples to show you. I do have images, but at this time cannot share them because those catalogs are privately owned. They will be the #50 and #411 jugs. Most of the rest are either here or we have attempted line drawings.

#7 jug, 11-1/2" tall, $95-130.

## #7 Tankard

### Crystal

Without a doubt the most fantastic tankard or pitcher ever made by Central or any other glassmaker is the #7 tankard. The best metals for the glass, and the best craftsmanship in the production and finishing work, make for a very beautiful product. It is 11-1/2-inches tall with a polished bottom and cut rayed base with an applied handle. The special cuts around the top and bottom will vary by width and height, and so will change the number of such treatments. The treatment on this piece is called Cut 174.

Imagine 75 years ago bringing this beauty into a room and serving your guests. Better yet, imagine serving your guests some iced lemonade from this fantastic example today.

## #11 Jug & Cover

### Crystal 80 oz.

The covered jugs by CGW are just fantastic crystal examples of the company's work. This blank was probably first seen around the turn of the century and would continue in service well into the 1920s.

#11 covered jug, 80 oz., without etch, $25-35; etched with Thistle etch #10, $225.

## #21 Jug

### Crystal

Example of the #21 jug shown measures 8-1/2-inches tall. It also has an applied handle and will not have been made with a cover.

#21 wide base jug without etch, $15-20 without etch.

## #32 Jug 64oz

### Crystal

The #32 is one of the more commonly found jugs made by Central. As in other crystal jugs of this style, they would have been made around the turn of the century up to the late '20s. The little two quart squatty pitcher would lend itself well to just about anything from ice water to lemonade. There will be no cover for this style of jug.

#32 squatty jugs, 64 oz., 6" tall, without etch $10-15.

## #50 Jug

### Crystal

While looking like pitchers or jugs made by all companies of the time, this is what Central's #50 jug looks like from a drawing.

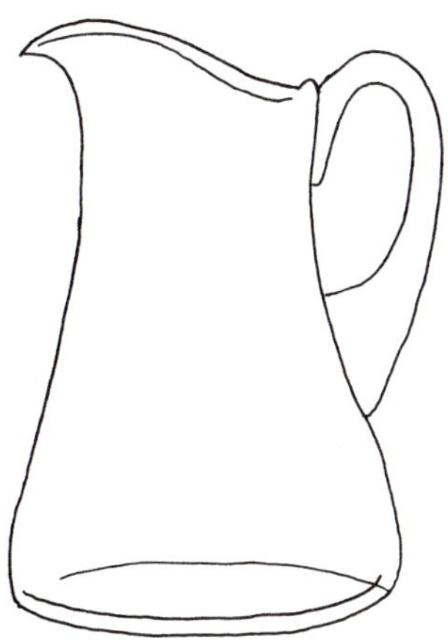

#50 Pitcher, drawing.

# #411 Jug

### Crystal

Example of the #411 jug or pitcher with an applied handle, no cover on this item. This jug has a squatty bottom with a narrow center widening toward the top with a nice pour lip. Jug measures 8-1/2-inches tall.

#411 pitcher, 8-1/2" tall, 75 oz., without etch $10-15.

# #1419 Tankard

### Tankard Crystal

This tankard, which will also have been produced by many other glass houses, measures 8-inches tall by 5-inches across the base, and has an opening of 3-3/8-inches. There is a highly polished pontil in the center of the base, and a handle that was applied. This tankard is one of many lines that evolved from the Chippendale line and continued in use for many years.

#1419 tankard, 8-1/2" tall, without etch $12-15.

# #1428 Pitcher

### Crystal, green, rose, orchid

The very deco 1428 line, according to catalogs, is to be found in all these great colors. So who's hoarding them? Until recently I could not even find stemware in anything but crystal or orchid tints. A recent find of the sherbet from the 1428 line in pink does hold great promise that we will find this jug and stems in green as well as amber. Jug images can be found in the Morgan etch section.

# Unknown Jug

I wanted to add this jug by photo and also from the old trade journal copy because other companies made it as well.

Unknown line number pitcher, $10-15 without etch.

# #2001 Jug & Cover

### Crystal or crystal with gold

Photo of the 2001 covered jug, this one has a gold trimmed lid.

#2001 covered jug with gold highlights top.
Price is for examples without etching, $35-40.

Trade journal copy showing unknown jug, top right, as well as other items of interest.

# Etchings by Central Glass Works

What follows are the etchings we know to be CGW's products.

## Etch #5 Scott's Morning Glory

### Colors: rose, green, amber, orchid tints, and crystal

Although only listed by an etch number in its humble beginnings, Scott's Morning Glory gets its name from Nathan Bay Scott, President and one of the founders of the re-emerged Central Glass Works company in 1896. Scott, a soldier in the Civil War and Statesman in West Virginia, is credited for giving Central Glass Works their rebirth. The etch #5 pattern, homage to Scott's being the most influential person in the company's history, gets its place in history as one of Central's most beautifully etched wares. The pattern has been found in most of the colors made by Central including Orchid Tints. And if memory serves me right, it has been found in black, which would be an exciting find.

Scott's Morning Glory will be found on many blanks ranging from the simple #112 plain line to the exotic #1428 deco line.

Etch #5, Scott's Morning Glory tankard set, tankard and 8 tumblers, $475-500.

Etch #5, Scott's Morning Glory #1428 wine in Orchid Tints color, $75-95.

Etch #5, Scott's Morning Glory tapered cordial, $45-50.

Etch #5, Scott's Morning Glory #112 saucer champagne, 4-1/2" tall, 3-5/8" top, 2-7/8" base, $18-22.

Scott's Morning Glory, Etch #5 close-up.

Scott's Morning Glory, Etch #5, 7-1/2" salad plate, $15-20.

Scott's Morning Glory Etch #5, #490 line saucer champagne, 5-1/2 oz., 4-11/16" tall, 3-7/8" top, amber, $ 22-25.

Scott's Morning Glory, Etch #5, #43 cone footed tumbler in amber, 4-5/8" tall, 3-3/4" top, 10 oz., $25-30.

Scott's Morning Glory Etch #5, #490 wine, 4-7/8" tall, 2-1/2 top, 3 oz., in amber, $25-30.

Scott's Morning Glory Etch #5, #301 table tumbler, 10 oz., $20-22.

Scott's Morning Glory Etch #5, close-up of etch on a tumbler.

Scott's Morning Glory Etch #5, #1422 sherbet and water goblets in rose color, $25-30.

# Etch #6 Grape

### Crystal only to date

How do you tell Central's Grape pattern from the other grape etches out there? Simple! Look at the bunch of grapes hanging low and to the center of the pattern; on one of the clusters there will be a cursive E to the left of the bunch. Now, that same set of grapes will be attached to the vine by opposing hangers that look strangely enough like fine wire ornament hangers. See the pattern close up.

This etch will be another that will cause controversy between the collectors of CGW products and the FRY people. I believe this etch to have originated with FRY in their Rochester Tumbler Company holding before the plant becoming part of the National Glass Company Combine takeovers and renaming of the plant to Rochester Tumbler Works. See more on this in the section on the Glass Company Takeovers / Combines.

This is one of Central's older patterns and will be found with crude or not so well defined plate etchings. The latter examples seem to be of a higher quality. Etch 6 has only been reported or found in crystal at the time of this printing. I have not personally seen any dual plate etchings in grape but would not be surprised to find some one day.

Etch #6 Grape saucer champagne, #528, 6 oz., 4-3/4" tall, $18-25, & sherbet #112, 6 oz., 3-1/2 tall, $15-20.

Etch #6 Grape #112, 9 oz., 6-1/4" tall water goblet, $20-25.

Etch #6 Grape, #1269 grape fruit, 6-11/16" tall, 5-1/4" top, base 3-13/16", $35-45.

Etch #6 Grape cereal bowl, 2-15/16" tall, 4-7/8" top, $22-25.

Etch #6 Grape, etch close-up.

Etch #6 Grape, water goblet, 9 oz., 6-1/2" tall, $20-25.

Etch #6 Grape, water goblet, 9 oz., 6-1/8" tall, $20-25.

Etch #6 Grape #1419 tankard, $50-60.

# Etch #7 Greek

### Crystal only to date

Greek, it is said, is the factory name for this etch, although I have never seen it in a catalog as such. Etch 7 is the only way I have ever seen this pattern named in reference by the company. This will be one of the early patterns for Central and is only found in crystal and truly represents the etchings of that time period in American glassware. While I can't prove that this pattern was made very early on, I do have three #112 wine stems in crystal that fluoresce well in black light, and all of the other examples that represent items made in the late teens and twenties (stem lines, etc.) do not. I do recall an article that the late Jerry Gallagher of Morgantown fame wrote in a monthly glass paper back in 1991, on Greek or Hanging Star as it had been called up to that point. In that article he had pointed out that the pattern that had been attributed most often to Morgantown was actually Central's etch #7 or Greek. Thanks posthumously to Jerry for pointing us in the right direction.

I have to believe the usual items will be found, as this is a long produced line with many pieces but will add prices for items that I have, or have seen at shows or markets. Note there are two sizes of cruets; one looks like it could be a syrup with higher arched shoulders (little neck area) and the other like the other cruets in the Central lines.

Etch #7 Greek, #1241 saucer champagne, ht. 4-1/2", top 3-3/8", base 2-7/8", $20-25.

Etch #7 Greek #112 claret, 4 oz., 3-13/16" tall, $15-18.

Etch #7 Greek, #1241-1/2, 11 oz. goblet, 6-1/2" tall, 2-13/16" top, 3-1/8" base, $20-25.

Etch #7 Greek #530, 16 oz. tumbler, 5-5/8" tall, 4-1/8" top, $25-28.

Etch #7 Greek, 6-3/8" wide, 1" tall, sherbet or saucer champagne liner plate, $15-18.

Etch #7 Greek, #1135 4 oz. parfait, 4-7/8" tall, top 2-3/8", $25-30.

Etch #7 Greek #530 St. Regis tumbler, 9 oz. & #1096, 9 oz. tumbler, $20-25 each.

# Etch #10 Thistle

### Crystal or crystal with gold filled etch only

The Central Glass pattern Thistle or etch 10 evolved from the Rochester Tumbler Company. While speaking on the subject of Central Glass Works for the West Virginia Museum of American Glass's Gathering at Replacements Limited in 1998, a woman, who was either researching the Fry Glass Company or was a collector, approached me to explain an error that I had made during my lecture. I had stated that the Rochester Tumbler Company and Rochester Tumbler Works were one and the same, and that H.C. Fry had owned Rochester Tumbler Company, and somehow Central Glass Works had acquired the Tumbler Works plant after the Combine takeovers. After the lecture, the woman approached me to correct my error, stating that while H.C. Fry did own the Rochester Tumbler Company, it was not the same company as Rochester Tumbler Works. Not having all my research material with me at the time and forgetting for the moment all of the details, I, somewhat confused, begged her pardon and decided I would try to figure out where I remembered getting this confusing notion. Returning home to my notes made it all too clear. First thing to remember is that according to American Glass House Directories published during this time, there did not ever exist a Rochester Tumbler Company and a Rochester Tumbler Works at the same time. And, both companies were in the same city, Rochester, Pennsylvania.

The earliest information I found for this pattern was in the *Crockery and Glass Journal* ad for the Thistle pattern by Rochester Tumbler Works in 1907. The Rochester Tumbler Company in Rochester, Pennsylvania, was taken over by the National Glass Combine in 1899. (In the final days of the late 1800s, the National Glass Company attempted to organize all the American glass companies into a combine in the belief that as one company they would have a stronger voice with both the government, to control tariffs on foreign wares, and labor unions.) The following is a trade journal excerpt from the fourth week, of the eight-month, of 1899. In it, it lists the Rochester Tumbler Company as being one of the many companies, along with Fry, to enter the Combine, and I quote:

> The National was permanently organized by the election of H.C. Fry, president. H.C. Fry also was named in the board of directors. Further along in the report it also states that; each company will go forward with their business as heretofore. Each plant will retain its individual name with Works attached, as in Rochester Tumbler Company will become Rochester Tumbler Works!

In the trade journal reprint of the full page Thistle pattern ad from 1907, it shows the company logo at the top as The Old Rochester Quality. Also it clearly shows the etch number "10" and the shapes and sizes we have seen in catalogs as Central Glass Works products.

Then, by 1908, we find Central Glass Works advertising the Deep Plate Etch 10 Thistle, and the logo for the company is The Old Central Quality. The logo is identical, except that just the company name has changed. The mystery to unfold now is how and when did Central Glass Works acquire the Tumbler Works. What were the details and exactly when did this take place? Remembering that Central was a novelty and barware maker that found themselves wanting to expand farther into the tableware market after the turn of the last century. They not only started and created new lines themselves but acquired tableware lines from other companies as well.

Many of Central's lines are confused with that of the Fry glass company and vise versa. Now we know why. Central will (may) have acquired more than just one line from the Rochester in their acquisition of the Tumbler Works and its Logo. I mean, when you acquire a plant or company, you don't get the logo and just one line, do you?

Now the real confusion starts when you add in all of the other companies that made this Thistle etched pattern! The closest match, or toughest to tell apart in the entire Thistle etches, is the Tiffin Special Thistle from the Central Thistle. I find no difference. I can show a Thistle Collector a piece of Tiffin Special Thistle and they'll swear to it as being Tiffin; then I remove my thumb from the base and uncover the Central Glass Works Sticker. Some will say that companies copied each other. If it sold well for Cambridge and Tiffin, Heisey would copy and run an identical pattern. In most cases this is true. I believe in the case of Central and Tiffin it was a little different story, as the companies shared too many patterns that are identical to the highest point.

Remember that under the control of the parent U.S. Glass Company, Tiffin (Factory R) and Central (Factory O) were sister companies during a tough time (late 1880s/ early 1890s) to be in the glass business. I believe strong business relationships evolved and joint ventures were commonplace between these two houses. If the managers of both houses were sitting at the table during board meetings with the US Glass Company, how can you not build a business relationship? Now, down the road a few years you have labor trouble with your glass plant, you make a call, and the molds are sent over to another plant and the line is produced there. How else can we explain so many similarities between Tiffin and Central? (This is the opinion and speculation of the author, me.)

Hopefully, as more information is uncovered from the archives we will learn more about this pattern and the history between the companies. What we do know is that the Central Glass Works Thistle Pattern was used in the White House as every day service for the President and Mrs. Harding in 1920.

And, this being the case and documented as so, where are the dinner plates in the Thistle or Etch 10 line? I have seen plates in smaller sizes but any plate bigger than 6-1/2-inches, I have never seen.

I do have a copy of a trade journal advertisement with the Etch #10 Thistle line, at the time being marketed by Rochester Tumbler Works. This, like most of my copies, will have some marking on them due to over excitement at finding any history on the company at all. So, while it looks like the Thistle etch came from Rochester, we can also figure all of the tumbler lines like the #530 will have originated there.

Etch #10 Thistle #1241-1/2 11 oz. goblet, 6-1/2" tall, $22-25.

## Thistle Etch #10, sizes where known, and prices

| Item | capacity | size | price |
|---|---|---|---|
| Ale #68 | 6 oz. | | ? |
| Coaster | | | $25 |
| Bowl fruit salad | | | $25 |
| Bowl #530 finger | | | $30 |
| Cup custard | | | $25 |
| Tumbler grape juice | 3 oz. | | $25 |
| Tumbler orange juice | 4 oz. | | $25 |
| Tumbler water | 6 or 8 oz. | | $30 |
| Tumbler handled tea | 10 oz. | | $95-125 |
| Stem cordial | 1 oz. | | $45 |
| Stem wine | 3 oz. | | $45 |
| Stem cocktail | 4 oz. | | $25 |
| Stem claret | 5 oz. | | $22 |
| Stem champagne saucer | 6 oz. | | $18 |
| Stem champagne flute | 6 oz. | | $35 |
| Stem champagne hollow | 6 oz. | | $125-130 |
| Stem water | 10 oz. | | $25 |
| Stem grapefruit | | 6-3/4 | $65 |
| Decanter/stopper #729 footed | | | $195 |
| Decanter/stopper #983 | | | $175 |
| Marmalade covered | 8 oz. | | $425-475 |
| Pitcher small | 16 oz. | | scarce |
| Pitcher #7 | | | scarce |
| Pitchers most | | | $75 |
| Pitchers covered | | | $225 |
| Teapot covered | | | scarce |

**Add $25-50 for items with the original sticker**

Etch #10 Thistle #530 flute champagne, 6-3/8" tall, 2-3/16" top, 2-1/4" base, $35.

Etch #10 Thistle #681 hollow stem champagne, 5-1/2" tall, $125-150.

Etch #10 Thistle #530 tumbler, 8 oz., $30.

Etch #10 Thistle #528 4 oz. cocktail, 3" tall, 2-11/16" top, $22-25.

Etch #10 Thistle #729 decanter with optic and cut 10, with rayed base, jeweled stopper, $195-225.

Etch #10 Thistle #528 5 oz. claret, 5-3/8" tall, 2-5/8" top, $22-25.

Etch #10 Thistle #528 saucer champagne, $15-18.

Etch #10 Thistle coaster, 4-3/8" wide, 11/16" tall, $20-25.

Etch #10 Thistle milk pitcher with cut 10, 4-5/8" tall, 16 oz., $275-400.

Etch #10 Thistle etch, close-up.

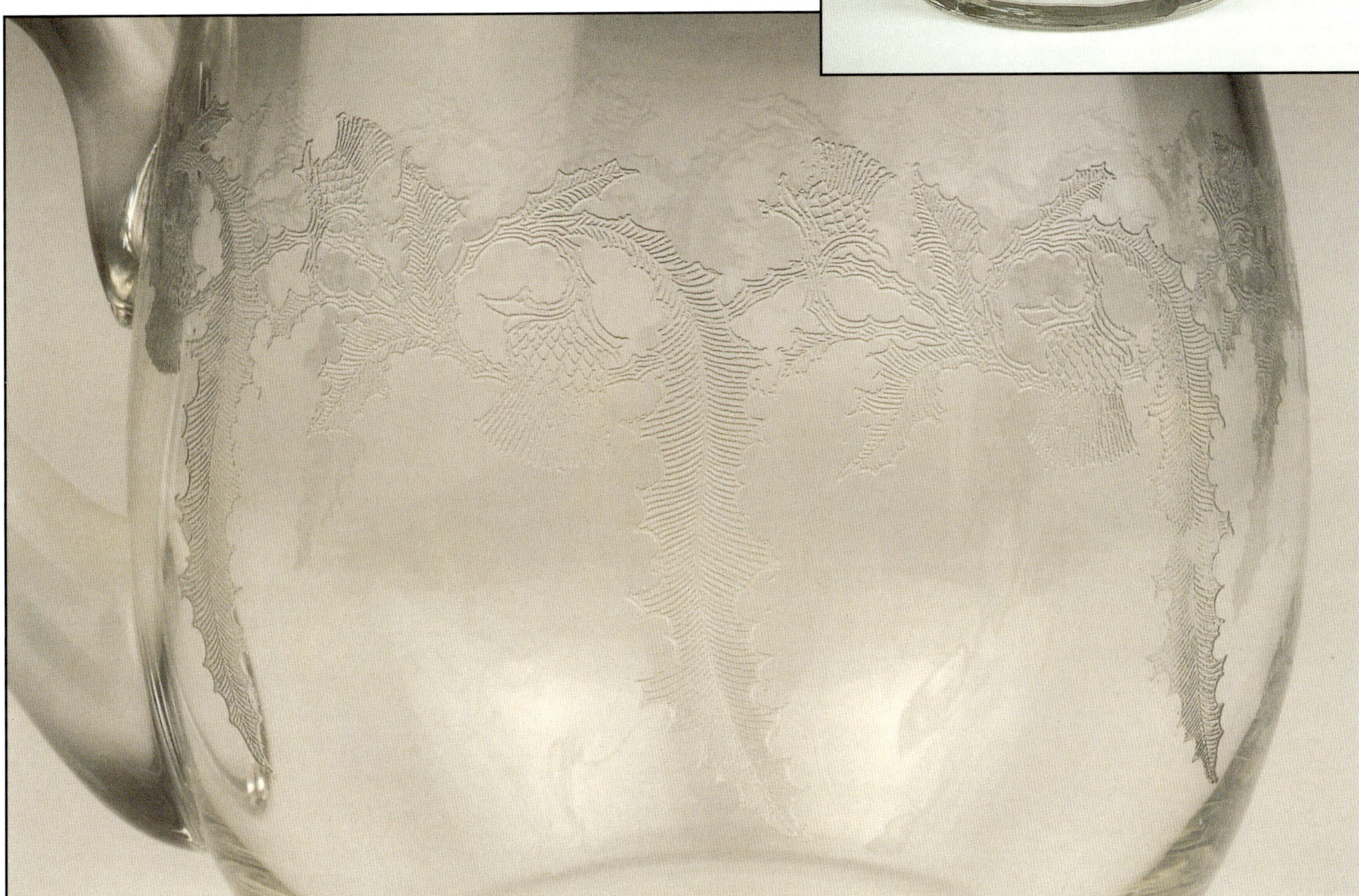

Etch #10 Thistle #2001 covered pitcher, $200-275.

Etch #10 Thistle #32 squatty jug, $75.

Etch #10 Thistle #2001 covered pitcher, detail of lid, $200-275.

Etch #10 Thistle #2001 covered pitcher, gold filled top, $200-275.

Trade journal copy of the etch #10 Thistle, c. 1907.

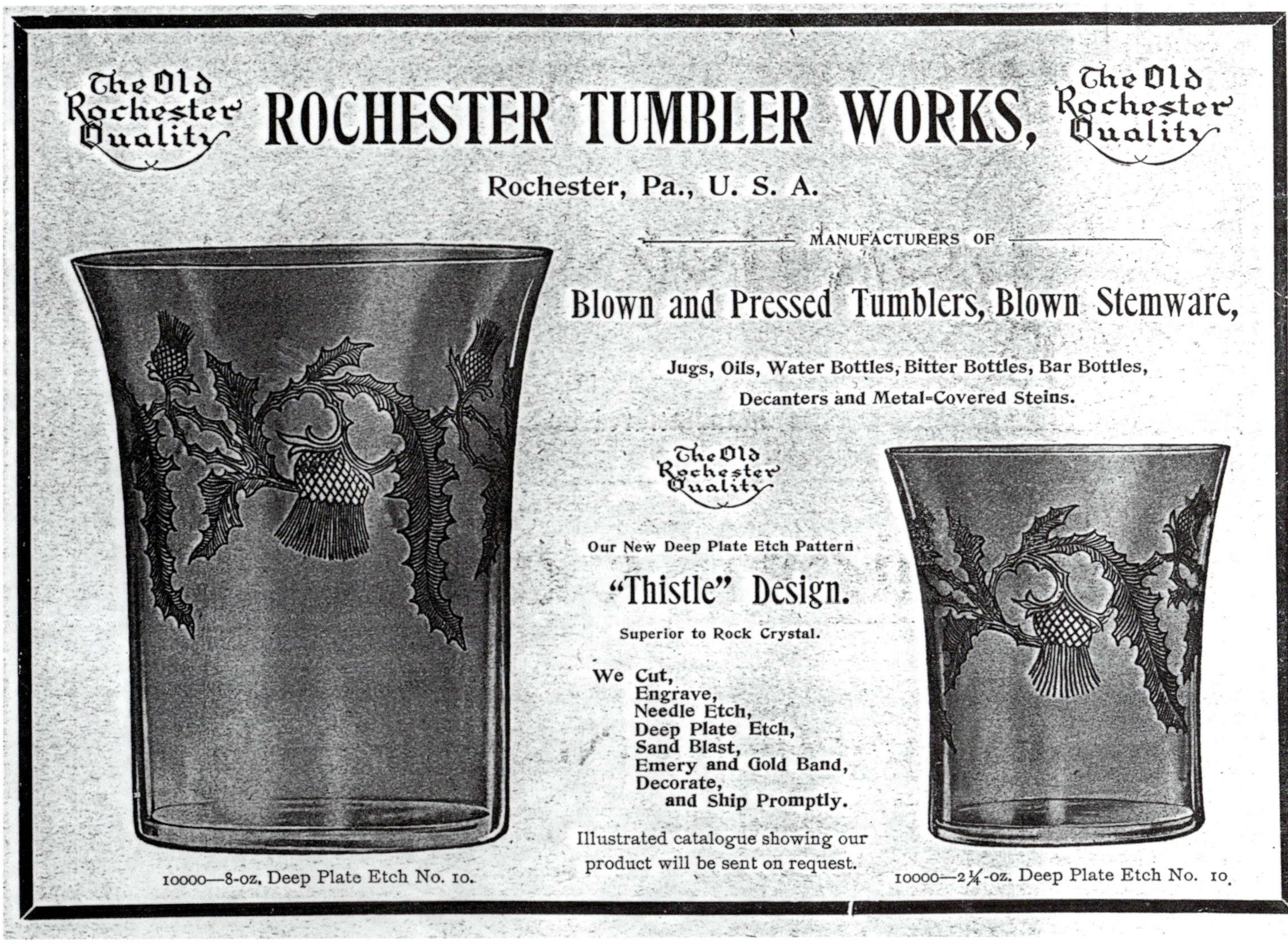

# Etch #11

## Crystal only to date

Now and again a piece will pop up here and there, but no real scores of etch 11 have surfaced. Since we know the example items shown are fragments of what would suggest a complete dinnerware line, we still need to find dinner plates and serving pieces. Or, was it made to compliment a china pattern we don't know of? We have been able to gather individual nut dishes, sherbets, and stems. There exists a catalog page of tumblers and a pitcher also. On an interesting note, all pieces have a very narrow optic.

Etch #11 sherbet, 6 oz., $8-10.

Etch #11, #112 small almond, 1-7/8" tall, top 2-1/2", base 2-1/16", $25.

Etch #11 3 oz. wine, 4-3/8" tall, 2-1/4" top, $12-15.

Etch #11 small wine, 3 oz., 3-11/16" tall, $15-18.

Etch #11 claret, 4-3/4" tall, 2-7/16" top, $15-18.

# Etch #14 del Solar's Wreath

### Crystal only to date

Finally finding out this pattern was in fact Central was an exciting discovery. I have had in my possession this #67 6-inch compote for over ten years waiting for the day I could attribute this etch to CGW. Now that this etch has its proper place in history, we should start seeing more of it coming out by name.

Some of the more recent finds are examples like the covered compote and covered lavender jar. What exciting finds these were, like no pieces I have seen yet by Central. I'm not sure if the covered compote is part of the #67 line or not because the catalog clearly states the sizes available in that line. I lean more toward it being part of the 2001 line. Regarding the lavender jar, I can find no catalog reference showing anything like it at all.

I have seen many pieces of this pattern over the years but have passed them up waiting to make sure that the etch did belong to Central, so pieces should be found with some searching. Again, don't pass up the open compotes because they look to be ground. There must have been a problem after the break off was removed as far as fire polishing, because all of these compotes have a fresh grind feel at the rim. On the other hand, if the top has been cut to the etch, then they probably have been cut too far by someone later. Listed is what we know, there will be more found.

| Item | capacity | height | price |
|---|---|---|---|
| Pitchers | | | $75 |
| Stem champagne hollow | 6 oz. | | $45 |
| Lavender jar | | | $185 |
| Compote 5" top | | 6" | $40 |
| Compote 6" top | | 6" | $40 |
| Compote covered | | | $195 |
| Cocktail #281 | | | $18 |
| Wine #281 | 3 oz. | | $22 |
| Sherbet #281 | 6 oz. | | $15 |
| Saucer champagne | 6-1/2 oz. | | $18 |
| Water goblet | 9 oz. | | $22 |
| Water goblet | 10 oz. | | $22 |

del Solar's Wreath or etch #14
Lavender Jar, 4-1/4" tall, $175-185.

del Solar's Wreath or etch #14 hollow stem champagne, 5-1/4" tall, $40-45.

del Solar's Wreath or etch #14, #67 6" tall, 6" top compote, $40.

del Solar's Wreath or etch #14, #281 water goblet, 6-3/16" tall, 9 oz., $20-25.

del Solar's Wreath or etch #14 tall footed compote, covered, probably 2001 line, $195.

## Etch #15 Bar & Garland

### Crystal only seen

While I do not have any representative pieces of this etch, I have a trade journal reprint listed under miscellaneous lines that shows the #720 stem with the etch #15 Bar and Garland pattern. Pieces known will be listed, and anything readers and searchers have found would be interesting to hear about. In the catalog shot, the #228 line of tumblers appears to have been made in the same fashion as the 301 lines, narrow bottom and flaring outward halfway up the side of the glass. This should have been a widely distributed pattern, but so far it's rarely been seen.

Etch #15 tumbler, *Photo Courtesy Larry Baker*, $28-30.

## Etch #18

### Crystal (by pattern age)

Looking like or close to Cambridge Marjorie, this is another elusive etching. Pieces of this pattern will be found, but every time I have seen it, the prices were out of this world for a pattern the seller could not properly attribute. Close-up images of the pattern will be found below. It looks like it will be found on the 301 line of tumblers, and if history repeats itself, Central will also have used the 1096 tumblers as well for this plate etch.

There are different styles of this etch as seen on different stems and tumblers. If space allows, you will be seeing both styles in the drawings.

Etch #18, as found on some items. *Drawing Courtesy Brad Schmidt.*

## Etch #16 Poppy

### Colors: unknown, but more than likely just crystal

Etch 16 is the name for Central's poppy pattern. While I have been unsuccessful in my search to find even a single bloom anywhere in this etch, it must exist somewhere out there. I have been looking for just a representative piece for at least ten years with absolutely no luck.

A single poppy in bloom with a single stem straight down out of the flower, winding around that stem are two other stems, one has a leaf and the other a start of a second bud. The catalog image looks like a small line. While there are no pieces to show, there is a great drawing of what the pattern looks like.

Etch #16 Poppy. *Drawing Courtesy Brad Schmidt.*

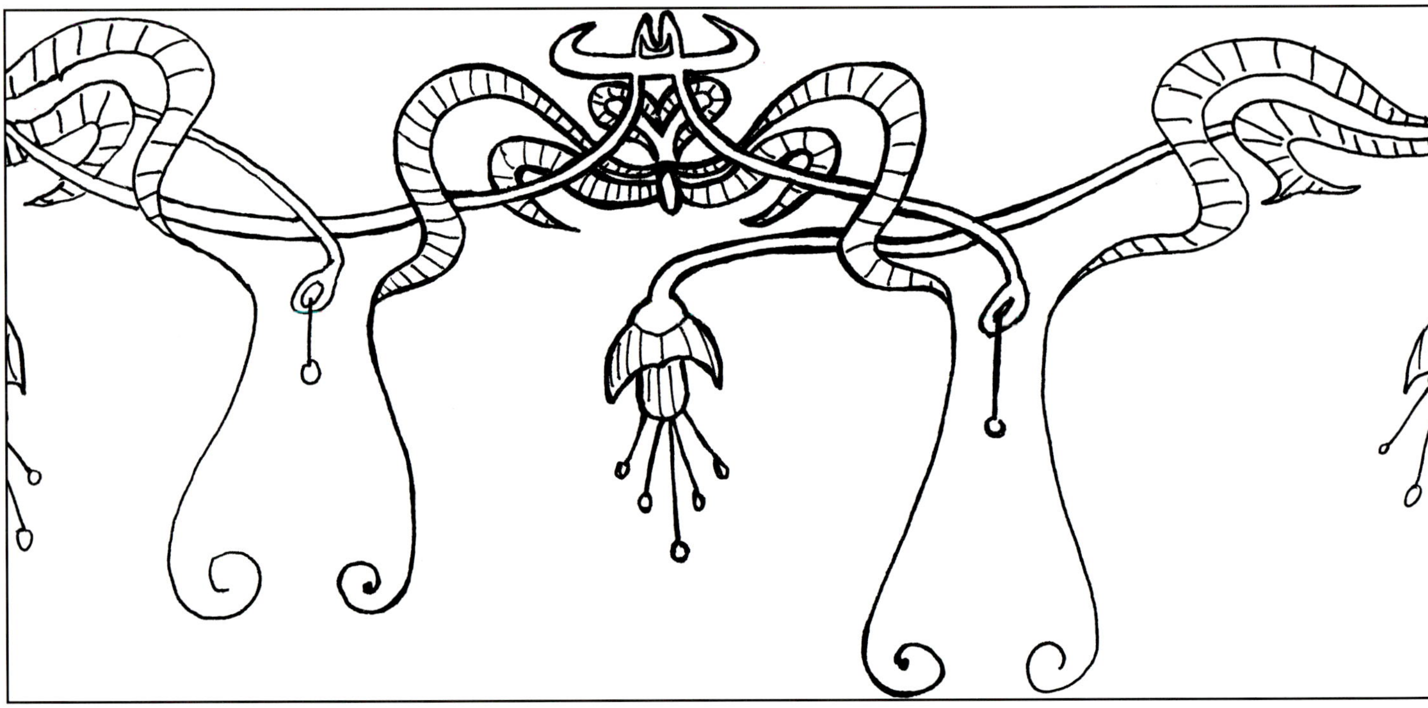

Etch #18, as found on other items. *Drawing Courtesy Brad Schmidt.*

## Etch #19 Oak

### Crystal and possibly crystal with gold

Although searching for the Oak pattern for years, it wasn't until 2003 that ANY of this etch found its way into the collection. Water goblets, sherbets, and handled ice tea glasses were discovered right here in the Midwest. Now we need to find more.

This pattern should not be hard to find as it was shown in the same catalog as the Thistle line and therefore should have been produced in the same pieces and quantities as Thistle. Etch 19 is a very well defined etch and could be the cause of its impossibility to find. I believe if pieces do show up they don't hang around long enough to gather dust.

As I have stated, pieces should be found in all the same blanks as the etch 10 or Thistle, but I'll list what I have for now and we'll go from there. Trade journal ad shows the release date of 1916.

Etch #19 Oak, #818 water goblet, 7-1/4" tall, 2-15/16" top, 10 oz., $30-35.

Etch #19 Oak, #818 saucer champagne, 5-3/8" tall, 3-3/8" top, 6 oz., $30-35.

Etch #19 Oak, #731 handled ice tea, 5-3/16" tall, 3-1/4" top, 11 oz., $65-75.

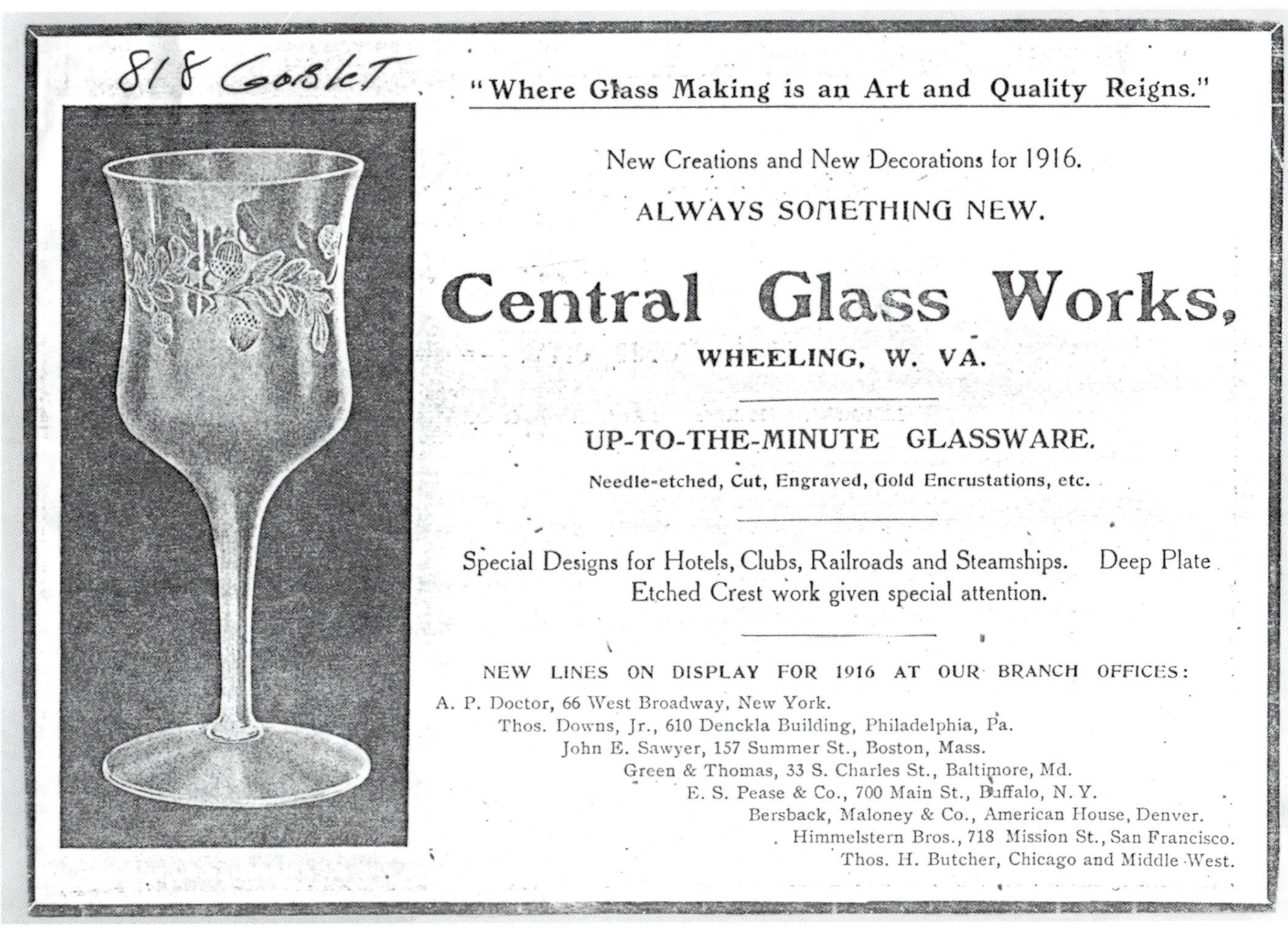

818 Goblet

"Where Glass Making is an Art and Quality Reigns."

New Creations and New Decorations for 1916.

ALWAYS SOMETHING NEW.

**Central Glass Works,**

**WHEELING, W. VA.**

**UP-TO-THE-MINUTE GLASSWARE.**

Needle-etched, Cut, Engraved, Gold Encrustations, etc.

Special Designs for Hotels, Clubs, Railroads and Steamships. Deep Plate Etched Crest work given special attention.

NEW LINES ON DISPLAY FOR 1916 AT OUR BRANCH OFFICES:

A. P. Doctor, 66 West Broadway, New York.
Thos. Downs, Jr., 610 Denckla Building, Philadelphia, Pa.
John E. Sawyer, 157 Summer St., Boston, Mass.
Green & Thomas, 33 S. Charles St., Baltimore, Md.
E. S. Pease & Co., 700 Main St., Buffalo, N. Y.
Bersback, Maloney & Co., American House, Denver.
Himmelstern Bros., 718 Mission St., San Francisco.
Thos. H. Butcher, Chicago and Middle West.

Etch #19 Oak, shown on the #818 line goblet, trade journal report dated 1916.

# Etch #22 Floral Trumpets

## Crystal

With an etch looking like four floral trumpets, this early etch will be found in crystal only. My first piece of this was an individual nut dish and was an exciting find, although like many first pieces, I paid way too much for it. But it's like that with all first pieces, you believe that another will never come by, so it's a "must have situation."

Since then, of course, water tumblers, stems, and even decanters have been found. Being made during the same time frame as the other late teen patterns, we should find many similar items. I'll list what I know of and you can expand on other findings.

A recent discovery of a very tall and elegant Roemer wine has been found with this etching.

| Item | capacity | height | price |
|---|---|---|---|
| Compote 5" top | | 6" | $22-25 |
| Compote 6" top | | 6" | $22-25 |
| Cordial #364 | 1 oz. | 3 1/2" | $22-25 |
| Sherbet #364 | 5 1/2 oz. | | $15-19 |
| Water #364 | 9 oz. | | $18-22 |
| Dish nut | | | $25 |
| Decanter/stopper | | | $75 |
| Decanter nite | | | $75 |
| Tumbler #1096 | 9 oz. | | $18-22 |
| Wine Roemer | 3-1/2 | 9" | $75-90 |

Etch #22 Floral Trumpets, #800 finger bowl, 2-1/4" tall, 4-5/8" top, $35-40.

Etch #22 Floral Trumpets, #112 cordial, 3-9/16" tall, 1 oz., $30-35.

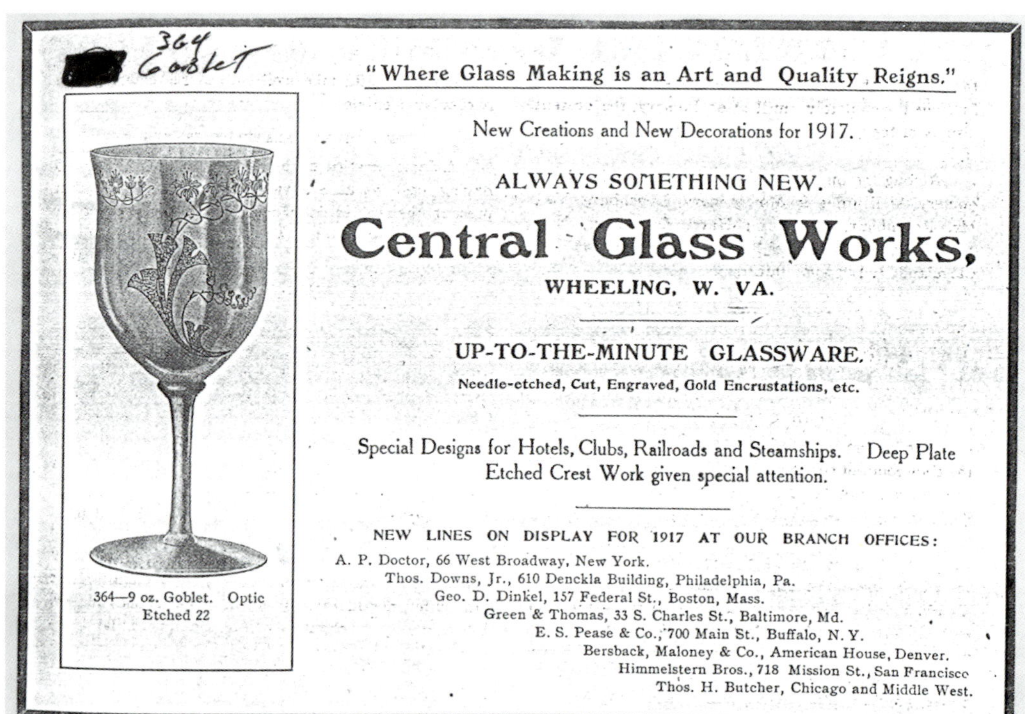


Etch #22 Floral Trumpets1917, trade journal copy.

# Etch #23 Roses

Etch #23 water goblet, 6-1/8" tall, 3-3/8" top, $35-40.

## Crystal and gold encrusted, also dual plate etched

The Etch 23 Roses pattern is superb in quality and craftsmanship. When found in the dual plate etched examples, the quality is second to none. Often sold or marketed as Fry Glass because of the quality, there exists the possibility that this will be another line that came over from the Rochester Tumbler Company. A listing on an Internet auction placed a Central Glass Works Etch #23 Roses bedside night set as a Fry Glass Company piece, which sold for over $150.

| Item | capacity | height | price |
|---|---|---|---|
| Candlestick | | | $45 |
| Baker's candy box | | | $125 |
| Candy box w/ gold | | | $175 |
| Console bowls | various shapes | | $75-90 |
| Compote | #67 | 6" tall 6" top | |
| Compote | #67 | 6" tall 5" top | |
| Compote | #7809 | 5" | |
| Compote | #7809 | 7" | |
| Compote | #7809 | 8" | |
| Decanter/tumble up | | | $200-225 |

**Should be found on many tumbler and stem lines.**

Etch #23 enhanced view of etch on goblet.

Etch #23 Baker's candy box, $125; with gold or dual plate etch, $175.

# Etch #51 Smetak

### Colors: crystal, rose, green, ebony, others, and with gold highlights

The Smetak etch looks to have an almost heart-shaped pair of fern stems with periwinkle flowers breaking off both sides. The etch will be found treated with gold and should be found in all the colors of the period. Pieces found in this etch so far are limited to accessory pieces, such as cheese and cracker sets, console bowls, and candy dishes, but no dinnerware or table service has been spotted, yet.

| Item | crystal | colors |
|---|---|---|
| Basket #2001 | $10-15 | $18-22 |
| Bon-bon #2005 | $12-15 | $22-24 |
| Baker's candy box | $25 | $45-55 |
| Cake plate #2002 | $15-20 | $20-22 |
| Candle stick #2000 | $18-25 | $22-30 |
| Candle stick #2020 | $25-30 | $40-50 |
| Console bowls #2000 | $22-25 | $25-30 |
| Console bowl #2014 | $22-25 | $25-30 |
| Console bowl #2025 | $25-30 | $30-40 |
| Lemon plate #2019 | $12-15 | $15-22 |
| Preserve #2019 | $12-15 | $18-22 |
| Salver #2002 | $15-20 | $25-32 |
| Mayonnaise set #2000 | $28-30 | $35-40 |
| Mayonnaise set #2001 | $28-30 | $35-40 |
| Cheese & Cracker #1103 | $18-22 | $25-30 |
| Pastry Tray #1435 | $18-20 | $22-25 |
| Compote #2005 | $15-20 | $22-25 |
| Compote #2000 | $15-22 | $22-25 |

Smetak or etch #51, on Baker's #2005 candy box in green, $50.

Smetak or etch #51, on #2000 amber candle, $22-30 each.

Smetak or etch #51, close-up.

# Etch #'s 61, 62 & 63

## Crystal and colors

Yes, we did skip ten etch numbers between #51 and #61. I would also like to know what they are, and where.

The next three etches will create some confusion, but we will be explaining or calling the etchings or treatments as they are shown in the catalogs. Etch 61 shows the basic etch that all three patterns will have in common. The number of the etch will vary by the amount of gold treatment the piece received around the medallion. Etch #61 will have the basic etch but can also have the wide gold border around the medallion. No treatment will be found on the medallion (etched area) itself. Etch 62 will have a gold filled medallion with a gold edge ring or two gold edge rings, one at the outer rim and one on the inside of the band. Etch 63 is totally gold trimmed or filled on the medallion and the band. So, simply put, the lower the number the lesser the amount of gold work done to the piece. The higher the number, the greater the amount gold work that would have been applied. I know this sounds silly, but after hours and hours spent pouring over the catalog copies, this will be the only difference in the etching or treatment numbers. All patterns or treatments can have the floral band under the medallion, but it is usually reserved for the larger pieces. These decorations or etches are only found on serving and accessory pieces. There haven't been any discoveries of stems or dinnerware items. Yet!

On the large oval serving bowl, the etch makes it all the way down the side of the bowl and onto the bottom area. It is simply magnificent, and it required a lot of extra care and craftsmanship to perform such work.

| **Item** | **size** | **crystal/ amber** | **green/ rose** | **black** |
|---|---|---|---|---|
| Candy Box | #2005 | $20-25 | $25-30 | $45-50 |
| Bon-bon | #2000 | $15-20 | $45-65 | |
| Comport | #2005 | $15-20 | $20-25 | |
| Candle | #2000 | $18-20 | $22-25 | |
| Candle | #2020 | $28-30 | $38-45 | $45-48 |
| Console Bowl | #2014 | $22-26 | $40-45 | |
| Console Bowl | #2025 10 1/2" | $55-65 | $60-70 | $70-75 |
| Console Bowl | #2025 13" | $60-70 | $65-75 | $95-110 |
| Console Bowl | #2000 var. shapes | $20-25 | $25-28 | |
| Console or fish bowl | #2025 | | $125-150 | |
| Bowl oval serving | | | $60-75 | |
| Lemon plate | #2019 | $22-25 | $25-30 | $40-45 |
| Preserve | #2019 | $22-25 | $25-30 | $42-45 |
| Salver | #2002 | $25-28 | $30-35 | |
| Mayonnaise | #'s2000/2001 | $30-35 | $35-40 | $75-90 |
| Pastry tray | fancy handle | | $65-75 | |
| Pastry Tray | #1435 | | | |
| Cheese & Cracker | #1103 | | | |
| Bell Bowl | #2002 | | | |
| Cake Plate | #2002 | | | |

**Etch 63, Full Gold Encrusted, Add 10%**

Etch #63, #2000 comport, close-up, $65.

Etch #63, #2000 line, comport and candlesticks in rose color, $100-110.

Etch #61 large #2002 oval bowl in rose color, 12-1/4" handle to handle, $60-75.

Etch #61, close-up.

Etch #61 on the 2025, 10 -1/2" footed bowl in amber, $65.

Etch #62, close-up.

Etch #62 #2002 mayo and liner plate in amber, $35-40.

Etch 61 filled border, close-up.

Etch #62 pastry tray (fancy handled) in rose color, $65-75.

Etch #62 #2014, 6 toed console bowl in rose color, $40-45.

Etch #62, #2025 line fish bowl in amber, *Photo Courtesy Larry Baker,* $125-150.

# Etch #401 Harding

## Colors: all so far except Golden Sapphire

Central's claim to fame pattern, Harding, is actually one of the few times Central named a depression era etch or pattern of glassware. Originally in its creation it was just given a line number. However, Harding will have been one of the longest produced patterns by the Central. The real original name for this pattern, as you will see in the trade journal advertisement of 1919, was Dragon.

Design etch #401 was probably created in the mid- to late mid-teens, and finally received a patent around 1919. But when President Harding, under pressure from the American Glass producers, wisely decided to use American made glassware on the tables of the White House for State Dinners, the pattern known as #401 received its historical name, Harding.

Cheaper foreign glassware was always a problem for the quality conscience American glass manufacturers, and inadequate tariff protection against these imported items made these products more attractive to the buying public. And, while I'm sure naming the pattern after the President gave the glass house a shot in the arm, without protection against the imports in the way of higher tariffs, any recovery was to be short lived. Remember, when looking at this pattern, that the Griffins face each other and that their tongues are out lapping at water spraying up from the fountain. If the Griffins are turned away from each other, that particular etch is a pattern by Tiffin Glass Company called Eldorado. For the record, in the press releases Central did refer to the etched figures as Dragons and not Griffins. (But, Dragons have short legs!) Harding has been found in all the colors made by Central except Golden Sapphire and Black ... so far. It was just discovered in Orchid Tints in 2001. So it would seem that pieces are being stored until the proper attribution has been made for this hard to find pattern.

This historical and very elegant pattern is greatly overlooked by collectors. Dealers, who realize that eventually this and other Central patterns will climb greatly in value due to their quality and scarcity, are buying pieces that do sell. The items that do get the most attention are the ice tubs and harder to find or rarely seen items. Bargain pieces right now are stems in any size in crystal and plates. A recent Internet auction purchase netted two crystal parfaits at $11 each! Having not even seen these pieces in years of collecting, I consider them to be quite a steal. Harding should be found on all of the tumblers made by CGW during this time period. This is also true of the stemware lines, except the 1470 line.

Please note if it is priced below in the chart it has been seen for sale, if not priced in the chart, it could, and should have been produced, so watch for those items.

| Item | size or number | crystal/ amber | rose/ green | orchid tints |
|---|---|---|---|---|
| Bon-bon | #2005 | $45-125 | $175-250 | |
| Bon-bon | #2019 | $45-75 | $65-80 | |
| Bon-bon | #2005 | | | |
| Bowl | #800 finger | $35-45 | | |
| Bowl grapefruit | #2005 | $150-175 | $275-325 | |
| Bowl cream soup | #2005 | $120-130 | $125-150 | |
| Bowl baked apple | #2005 | | | |
| Cake Plate 4 ftd. | $75-95 | | | |
| Candlesticks | #2000 | $110-125 | $125-175 | |
| Candy/Cover | #500 | $125 | $125/145 | |
| Compote | #67 5in top | | $275 | |
| Compote | #67 6in top | | | |
| Compote Grapefruit | 6-11/16 T x 5-1/4 W | $35-40 | | |
| Compote Grapefruit | 4-1/4 T x 5-1/4 W | $28-35 | | |
| Console bowl | #2000 various shapes | $35-70 | $80-150 | |
| Lily bowl | #2005 | $50-65 | $90-150 | |
| Creamer/Sugar | various lines | $75-100 | $90-125 | |
| Cup/Saucer | #2005 | $35-50 | | |
| Ice tub | 2002 | $250-300 | | |
| Ice Bucket | 4-1/4 deep/ 9" wide | $300-575 | $1100 | |
| Mayonnaise set | #2000 & 2001 | $90-125 | $125-150 | |
| Oil and Vinegar | | $375 | | |
| Parfait | 5-1/2 T 6 oz. | $22 | | |
| Stems | #112 Line | | | |
| Stems | #780 Line | $20-30 | $35-40 | |
| Stems | #1426 Spiral | $25-30 | $35-40 | |
| Stems | #1428 Line | | | $60-150 |
| Stems | #1434 Line | | $28-60 | |
| Stems | #1440 Line | | $30-65 | $50-85 |
| Stems | #1450 Line | | $75-125 | |
| Stems | #1451 Line | | | |
| Tumblers | #43 Line | | $75-80 | |
| Tumblers | #301 Line | | | |
| Tumblers | #492 Line | | | |
| Tumblers | #528 Line | | | |
| Tumblers | #530 Line St. Regis | $22-25 | | |
| Tumblers | #1096 line | | | |
| Tumblers | #2001 line | | | |
| Tumblers | #1447 ftd. | $35-40 | | |
| Pitchers or Jugs no cover | | $125-325 | | |
| Pitchers or Jugs covered | | | | |
| Pitcher | #1426 spiral | | | |
| Pitcher | #1428 | | | |

DEEP PLATE ETCHINGS

We have recently brought out a number of patterns absolutely new to glassware. These are designed to match types of dinnerware decorations now so popular. The Dragon design illustrated is typical. It is shown in a full line of stemware and tableware, and fully maintains the CENTRAL reputation for quality craftsmanship.

CENTRAL GLASS WORKS

Wheeling, W. Va.

Trade journal release for the "Dragon design," from *Crockery and Glass Journal*, c. 1919.

Harding etch #401, #780 crystal water goblet, $20-30.

Harding etch #401, #2005 cream soup in rose, $125-130.

Harding etch #401, #2005 cream soup in amber, $120-130.

Harding etch #401, #500
candy and cover, $125-145.

Harding etch #401, #43 12 oz. footed
water tumbler in green, $75-80.

Harding etch #401, #43 12 oz. footed
water tumbler in rose, $75-80.

Harding etch #401, #780 tall
saucer champagne, $20-30.

Harding etch #401, #67
compote, 6" tall, 5" top,
$250-300.

Harding etch #401, #800 finger bowl, $35-45.

Harding etch #401, #2005 cup and saucer, $125-150.

Harding etch #401, #780 tall water goblet, $20-30.

Harding etch #401, on #352 oyster cocktail in rose color, 3-1/2" tall, 3-1/8" top, 2-7/16" base, $75-95.

Harding etch #401, 7-1/2" salad plate in green, $25-35.

Harding etch #401, #2005 grapefruit in green, 7-3/4" across, 1-1/4" tall, $275-325.

Harding etch #401, #1428 saucer champagne in Orchid Tints, 5" tall, 4" in top, $75.

Harding etch #401, #1210 5 oz. parfait, 5-5/8" tall, 2-5/8" top, $65-70.

Harding etch #401, #43 footed juice, 4-1/4" tall, 3" top, crystal/green, $50-60.

Harding etch #401, #1428 wine in Orchid Tints, 5-3/16" tall, 3" top, $135.

Harding etch #401, #1445 12 oz. table tumbler, $35-40.

Harding etch #401, #1450 ice tea tumbler, 6-1/4" tall, 3-1/4" top, crystal/ black, $125.

Harding etch #401, #530 St. Regis table tumblers, 4-3/4" tall, 3" top, 10 oz., $25; 3-3/4", 2-1/2" top, 4 oz., $25.

Harding etch #401 bead stem water goblet, 7" tall, 3-3/8" top, crystal/green, $35-50.

Harding etch #401 sherbets, #780 in rose color, 4-1/4" tall, 3-3/4" top, $75-90; #490 in crystal, 4-1/2" tall, 3-5/8" top, $35-50.

Harding etch #401, #2000 candles in crystal, $110-125.

**Right:**
Harding etch #401 oil and vinegar bottle, $375.

**Far right:**
Harding etch jug, Tiffin style, amber, $325 *Courtesy Neil and Ethel Unger.*

**Below:**
Harding etch #401, #2005 footed low compotes, rose, green, and amber, $125-250 depending on color: amber: $125; rose/green: $250.

# Etch #402

### Crystal only

This pattern will be one of the earlier etched patterns by CGW and there are needle etched and raised etch examples. These early pieces exhibit very crude decorated examples of the 402 etch, but the glass is of a very high quality being very light and fragile. Later plate etched examples are well defined and the blanks slightly more durable. To date the pattern has only been found in crystal and only in stemware and a pitcher. Heisey did make a similar pattern, see the differences between the two in the Look-A-Likes chapter. The 402 etch should be found in all the line numbers that were made during the early 1900s up to the early to mid-1920s.

Etch #402 wine, 5-1/8" tall, 2-1/8" top, $12-15.

Etch #402 cordial, 3-1/2" tall, 1-1/2" top, $20-22.

Etch #402, close-up.

Etch #402 pitcher, $35-50.

# Etch #404 Leaf & Border

Etch #404 Leaf, Urn, & Border sherbet dish, $20-25.

## Crystal

Leaf & Border is yet another etch that has not be found without some searching. The only piece I have found so far is a #364 sherbet. There were others available for purchase at the same price, but they were a little on the pricey side for an unknown obscure example. And so far further examples have not appeared. Trying to describe the etching on this piece is just about as difficult as finding the pieces. The etch on the top band has a sort of Greek Key look with a single laurel vine running through the middle. There is also a saw tooth band above and below the Greek Key design. Further down in the etch we find a fan paddle-shaped leaf design which sits next to a fern or plant stand, and from that stand, a floral scroll out both sides with a plume coming up through the middle which rises above the floral scroll. This design is repeated around the piece numerous times. In fact I count six paddles and fern stands on the low sherbet.

The glass is very well made, crystal clear, and the etching very well done. Good strong design. And now that you know exactly what it looks like, you will be able to find all those pieces that I have not been able to locate.

Catalog shows high and low sherbets as well as the table tumblers and water goblets. Looks like it will be a very limited line.

Etch #404 Leaf, Urn, & Border etch, close-up.

# Etch #405 Greek Key and Swag

Etch #405, Greek Key and Swag #32 jug, $35.

## Crystal to date

I have finally found some #405 to add to the reference. This will be a limited run and so far only pitchers and tumblers have been found. While the catalog shot shows only the 1096 tumbler, I have examples to share that are the St. Regis or 530 line. So far all we know or have seen are examples in crystal. Listed or known pieces are below.

| Item | size or line # | price |
|---|---|---|
| Sherbet | #492 5 oz. | |
| Saucer champagne | #492 6 oz. | |
| Water goblet | #492 9 oz. | |
| Tumbler | #1096 9 oz. | |
| Tumblers | #530 St. Regis | $13-15 |
| Squatty jug | #32 | $35 |

Etch #405, Greek Key and Swag wines with original stickers, 4-1/2" tall, 2-3/8" top, *Courtesy Charles Griggs*, $25-30

Etch #405, Greek Key and Swag, #530 St. Regis tumbler, 10 oz., $15-18.

# Etch #408 Linda

Linda etch #408 milk pitcher, 6-3/4" tall, $95.

### Crystal and blue found to date, other colors may be out there

There will be two types of the Linda or etch 408 found. The first design is the full etch with the band across the top of the piece with a cross-buck design filling in the band. The second style simply leaves off the band. This style seems to be more prevalent on stemware and smaller pieces. The most exciting find to date is the small milk pitcher. A fabulous piece holding about one quart.

This should be a pretty good sized line as the catalog shows pitchers, bowls, compotes, and plates.

| Item | size or line # | price |
|---|---|---|
| Bowl finger & liner | #800 | |
| Compote | #67 6" t 6" w | |
| Compote | #67 6" t 5" w | |
| Stems | various blanks | $25-70 |
| Pitcher | #411 | |
| Milk pitcher | | $95 |

Linda etch #408, close-up.

# Etch #409

### Colors: crystal and unknown if any other

Etch #409 will be another pattern held and kept very expensive by sellers and usually referred to as Fostoria. I have never seen this pattern properly attributed to Central Glass Works. It should be found on all the lines produced during this time period. Items like the #530 tumblers, #67 compotes, finger bowls, and jugs will be found. The drawing below is very representative of the actual etching.

Etch #409. *Drawing Courtesy Brad Schmidt.*

# Etch #410 Balda

### Colors: Crystal, blue, amber, rose, green, orchid tints, and ebony

Etch 410 is without a doubt the largest pattern ever produced by Central Glass Works, covering almost all blanks used by the company during, just before, and after the Great Depression. Complete dinnerware lines, bowls of all shapes and sizes, all stem and tumbler lines of the era, candlesticks, and vanity items will be found. Also etch 410 will be the longest produced pattern by CGW, being manufactured well in to the late 1930s.

Etch 410 received its name not from the company but from a gentleman named Ed Trindle, who penned the pattern after the designer who created it, Joe Balda.

Important to note, there are two styles of the 410 etch, with and without the extra floral bow under the main pattern. Also, there will be two different qualities of the etch from an earlier thicker and fuller pattern of etch, to the later more well defined, lean and trim examples found more in to the depression era or later 1920s and into the '30s. Balda has been seen in all of the basic company colors with the exception of Golden Sapphire.

To give complete coverage to all pieces made in this etch would require a book in itself, so I'll try to give you a quick breakdown of what you will find.

| Item | line | capacity | size | crystal/ amber | rose/ green blue | orchid/ ebony/ |
|---|---|---|---|---|---|---|
| Bowls, console | | | | $20-45 | $40-110 | $75 |
| Bowl floral w/ metal frog | | | | $100 | | |
| Bowl cream soup | 2005 | | | $25-55 | $65-75 | |
| Bowl finger | 800 | | | $25-35 | | |
| Bowl soup | 2005 | | | $35-60 | $65-95 | |
| Bowl ruffled/ crimped | | | 10" | $70-95 | | |
| Bowl celery | 1450 | | 10" | $40-65 | | |
| Candle | 2000 | | | $25-50 | $55-75 | |
| Candle | octagon ball | | | | $35-55 | $55-90 |
| Candy | 500 | | | $75-90 | $95-125 | |
| Cheese & Cracker | 1103 | | | $35-50 | $55-95 | $75-90 |
| Compote | #67 | | 5 or 6" | | | |
| Creamer/Sugar | | | | | $95-125 | |
| Cup & Saucer | 2005 | | | $25-35 | $35-55 | $75 |
| Decanter w/ stopper | 1428 | | | $35-55 | $95-125 | $95-125 |
| Shakers pr | 2001 | | | $75-125 | $175-225 | |
| Tray ctr hand sandwich | | | | $35-55 | $45-95 | |
| Mayonnaise/ liner/spoon | 2000/ 2001 | | | $30-55 | $75-90 | |
| Pitcher colored handle | | | | $75-90 | | |
| Pitcher | #1426 | | | | | |
| Pitcher | #32 | | | $45-65 | | |
| Plate bread | | | 6 5/16" | $10-15 | $15-20 | $25-45 |
| Plate salad | | | 7-1/2" | $10-15 | $30-45 | $45-95 |
| Plate lunch | | | 8-11/16" | $12-20 | $30-45 | $45-95 |
| Plate dinner | | | | $25-30 | $35-50 | $50-75 |
| Platter 4 ft. round | | | 11" | $25-30 | $35-50 | $45-60 |
| Platter | | | 12" | | | |
| Stems | #780 | | | $15-25 | $35-50 | $95-125 |
| Stems | #818 | | | | | |
| Stems | #1426 | | | $15-25 | $25-35 | $55-95 |
| Stems | #1428 | | | | $75-90 | $50-90 |
| Stems | #1434 | | | $25-30 | $75-90 | $75-90 |
| Stems | #1440 | | | $30-50 | $90-125 | |
| Stems | #1447 | | | | | |
| Stems | #1900 | | | | | |
| Tumblers | #530 St. Regis | | | $25-35 | | |
| Tumblers | #1428 | | | | | $35-55 |
| Tumblers | #1434 | | | | $30-50 | |
| Tumblers | #1440 | | | | | |
| Vase fan | | | | $50-75 | $75-125 | |
| Vase | #2001 | | 8" flip | $35-50 | $75-100 | $95-125 |
| Vase tall | | | 9" | $25-65 | | |

Balda etch on #1426 tall water goblets in rose/crystal, $25-35.

Balda etch on #1428 sherbet in rose color, $75-90.

Balda etch on #1440 saucer champagne in rose color, $125.

Balda etch on #1440 water goblet, green/crystal, $95.

Balda etch on #1900 Winslow line, tall water goblet, crystal, $200-225.

Balda etch on #1447 walnut stem, tall water goblet, rose/ crystal, $200-225.

Balda etch on #500 covered candy, green, $95-125.

Balda etch on #2000 line candles, amber, each $35-50.

Balda etch on #2005 cups and saucers, crystal, $25-35; Orchid Tints, $75.

Balda etch on 7-1/2" salad plates, blue, $85; Orchid Tints, $45.

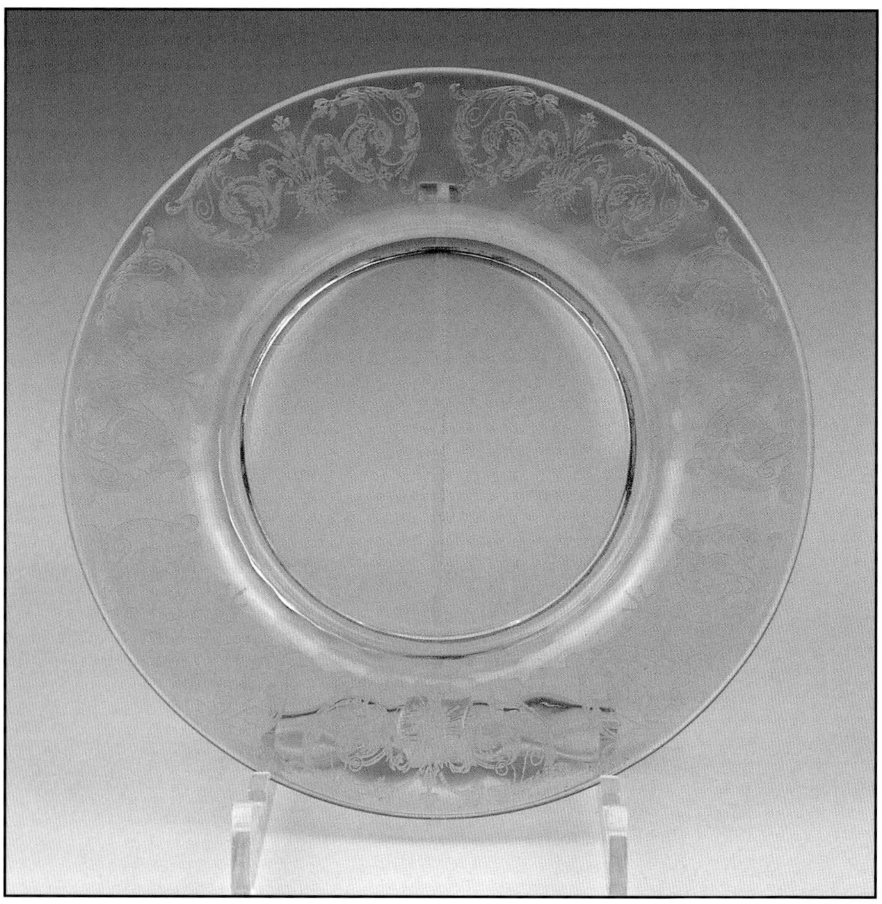

Balda etch on 6-5/16" bread and butter plate, in Orchid Tints color, $45.

Balda etch on 8-11/16" luncheon plate in rose color, $45.

Balda etch on #1428 sherbet, $50-60; tall water goblets, $85-90.

Balda etch on #818 saucer champagne, in blue, $195-225.

Balda etch, close-up showing extra floral pattern found on earlier produced pieces.

Balda etch on #1420 saucer champagne, 6 oz., 4-9/16" tall, 3-13/16" top, crystal, $18-25.

# Etch #411 Swag & Dangle

## Colors: Crystal and should be found in blue

This is another full line of stemware, pitchers, plates, compotes, and bowls that will share a 1920 patent date with many of CGW's other depression era patterns that is not readily found. I have seen this etch in years past but could not attribute it to Central until just recently. For that reason, I have just the one example, and an etch close-up to get us searching. Etch #411 will share many of the features of the Linda or #408 etch, but will have a different border design filled with laurel type leaves, and will also have urns filled with flowers. These two patterns in my opinion should mix fairly well if you have trouble finding enough of just the one design.

Etch #411, saucer champagne, crystal, $10-12.

Etch #411, close-up on sherbet stem.

# Etch #412 Morgan

### Colors: all except Golden Sapphire

This pattern is not only popular with depression era glass collectors but with fairy collectors as well. I have seen the histories of those who collect fairy items bidding in online auctions and while they bid on cute little fairy novelties, their collections have crossed over into the glass world as well. I believe these collectors have caused this pattern to rise quickly in prices.

While most Heisey, Cambridge, and other great companies have stems and tumblers that range from thirty to ninety dollars each, similar Morgan stems have reached two hundred dollars a piece. And it seems the common or average price is ninety-five dollars for each stem. The bad news here is I do not believe prices will get any better for this pattern that is already difficult to find. While prices do fluctuate at shows and online auctions, there exists too much competition for such a scarce example of Central's work.

The earliest we see Morgan is in the U.S. Patent and Copyright date of 1919. Later this pattern will be advertised in *Crockery and Glass Journal* as the pattern Central presented to Governor Morgan of Wheeling, West Virginia, as the table service for the Executive Mansion. Governor Morgan was in fact following the lead of President Harding, who wanted to do away with foreign glassware on the dining table of the White House. The fact that the American glass houses were suffering from high operating costs and troubles associated with labor unions must have made it tough for the President with the business community to continue using the cheaper foreign products.

I am convinced this pattern was actually inspired by two mischievous little girls in Great Britain in 1917 (read about The Cottingly Fairy's) who, with the use of a camera belonging to the father of one of the girls, turned the whole world upside down. The report that these two children had indeed caught real fairies at play in the woods by their home and photographed them brought media attention from around the world to their door. While many disputed the images as a hoax, the famous author Sir Arthur Conan Doyle would write articles claming the pictures were in fact real. Thus the fairy craze would sweep over England and carry abroad. Every day, regular curious folks loaded with camera equipment and professional photographers from around the globe would rush to the woods to capture an image of a real fairy. This came at a time when the world needed a spiritual lift. World War I had just ended.

While many believed they had nothing left to hope for, this glimpse, real or not, lifted them to rejoice in the world of fairies and angels and the powers of the heavens being real, real enough to give them something to hold on to, something to believe in, something physical to grab and embrace. It would appear that J. Balda (a freelance pattern designer) who created the 412 etch we now call Morgan, must have been just slightly more than fascinated with Fairies and the Fairy craze as he also, I believe, is attributed with the Heisey Renaissance etch that is very similar to the 412 etch. (See the Look-a-Likes section.)

Central Glass was shipped heavily to Great Britain, so it should be no surprise to find Central products in England and surrounding countries, as well as Australia. I have been seeing pieces of Morgan as well as other Central products showing up on Internet auctions from sellers abroad, which supports this belief.

Morgan, as with other Central products, is difficult to collect. My advice is, if you see a piece, grab it. Its value seems to just be going up, as its popularity gains momentum.

Prices for crystal are the most reasonable, with Orchid Tints and Blue commanding the highest dollars. While the Pamona Green is a nicer color, it seems to be tied with the rose color for pricing. Dinner plates are very scarce in any color and in crystal. Stems are the most commonly found and odd serving or accessory pieces are next. Many opted for plates in china patterns at this time and the stems and serving or occasional pieces would be used to compliment the settings. Luncheon plates are also found in crystal and pink fairly easily. Central claims to have started the use and distribution of the luncheon plate before any other glass company (trade journal report), and they are plentiful. I will attempt to cover what pieces can be found but space will be limited to all the different or individual stems found.

Keep in mind, Central was not marketed to the average glass buyers, but rather to, let's see how did they say it in their ads?, "Deep etched ware that affords the mistress in the well appointed home the utmost pride in its display to her guests". As you can see, they catered and marketed to a higher clientele for their etched wares. Because it was during such depressed times, average buyers could not afford these handmade gems and not many were sold. Pieces continue to escalate in price as small amounts find their way into today's market.

Be sure to check the top areas of the stemware and bowls, or any piece for that matter, for repairs or grinds. Central stems will have been fire polished to give them a slippery smooth feel to the top rim. In doing this, the stem would tend to sag slightly between the paneled optics in the bowl. Looking at the top of a factory-finished stem, it will appear somewhat uneven between these lines or panels. If it is not smooth and shiny to the eyes, try closing your eyes and feel with your fingertips. They should be smooth all the way around, not ground or beveled to the edge. That is the sign of repairs, and prices drop 50-70% for repaired stems or any other piece. This check holds true for all Central stemware except the #67 line of compotes, and the #780 **tall** saucer champagnes.

| Item | line | size | crystal | amber/ rose/ green | blue/ orchid/ ebony |
|---|---|---|---|---|---|
| Bowl finger | #800 | | $30 | | |
| Bowl fruit salad | #1470 | | | $145 | $175-225 |
| Bowls various console | | | $95 | $225-325 | $750-950 |
| Bowl 3 ftd. | dolphin ft. | | | $95-125 | |
| Bowl ruffled | | 10" | | $235 | |
| Bowl large w/ liner | 2002 | | | $550-625 | |
| Bowl mayo set | unknown line | | | $275 | |
| Bowl small | #2019 | | $75-90 | $95-125 | |
| Bowl lemon plt. | #2019 | | $65-75 | $95-125 | $175-325 |
| Bowl mayo set | #2019 | | | $325 | |
| Bowl mayo set | #2000 | | | $300-325 | |
| Bowl mayo set | #2001 | | | $300-325 | |
| Compote | #2005 | | $110 | $275 | $275-375 |
| Compote tall | #2005 | | | $250 | |
| Compote | #67 | 6t x 5w | | $395 | |
| Compote | #67 | 6t x 6w | | $750-800 | |
| Compote | #2000 | | | $175 | |
| Compote | #2005 | 6-3/4 w x 3-3/8 t | | $195-250 | |
| Candles | #2000 | | $225-275 | $275-350 | $1500-2500 |
| Candles octagon | | | | $195-225 | $250-325 |
| Candy covered diamond | | | | $425-500 | |
| Candy cone ftd. | #500 | | | $175-225 | $325-500 |
| Candy small covered | | | | $400-525 | |
| Creamer & Sugar | | | $175-225 | $250-375 | $375-550 |
| Cup & Saucer | | | $250-300 | $300-375 | $350-425 |
| Decanter | #1428 | | | $375-500 | $550-750 |
| Decanter set | w/tray & 6 shots | | | $995-1300 | $1100-1500 |
| Ice tub round | | | | $600-750 | |
| Ice tub rectangle | | | $995-1200 | $1175-1500 | $1500-1900 |
| Pitcher | #411 | | $1500 | | |
| Pitcher | crystal/ colored handle | 8-3/4 t | $375-425 | | |
| Pitcher | #1428 | | $1100-1300 | | $2500-3000 |
| Plate bread/ butter | | 6" | $40-50 | $40-50 | $70-90 |
| Plate salad | | 7" | $50-60 | $50-60 | $75-90 |
| Plate lunch | | 8" | $50-60 | $50-60 | $75-90 |
| Plate dinner | | 9-1/2 | scarce | scarce | scarce |
| Champagne | hollow stem | | $95-125 | | |
| Stems | 818 line | | $115-135 | $150-175 | |
| Stems | #1426 | | | $95-125 | |
| Stems | #1428 | | | $95-125 | $200-275 |
| Stems | single wafer separator | | $95-125 | $125-195 | $225-275 |
| Stems | #1434 line | | $125-175 | $195-225 | |
| Stems | #1440 line | | | $225-275 | |
| Tumblers | #530 | | $115-135 | | |
| Tumblers | #1445 | | | $225 | |
| Tumbler sherbet | #1450 | 6 oz. | $195-225 | | |
| Tumbler water | #1450 | 10 oz. | $225-250 | | |
| Tumblers | #1447 | | $105-115 | | $195-225 |
| Tray cheese/ cracker | #1103 | | | $175-225 | $200-250 |
| Tray pastry | #1435 | | | $275-300 | |
| Tray bon-bon | #2005 | | $75-90 | $150-195 | |
| Vanity | covered dresser tray | | | $650-725 | |
| Vase bud | #1320-168 | 10" | $175-225 | $295-475 | $350-450 |
| Vase | #2001 | 8" | | $2500-3000 | |
| Vase | tall thin | | | $500-650 | |
| Vase | Fan | | | $175-225 | $375-425 |
| Whipped cream dish | footed | | | $275 | $375 |

**Dual plate etch add 50%**

Advertisement March 6 1924
*Crockery and Glass Journal.*

Morgan etch #2019 bon-bon in black, $325.

Morgan etch #2001, 8" drape optic vase, $2500-3000.

Morgan etch #43, 2-3/4" oz. grape juice tumbler in rose, $175-200.

Morgan etch #1428 crystal pitcher, $1100-1300.

Morgan etch #1445 table tumblers, 12 oz. green/ crystal, $75-90; 10 oz. rose, $95-125.

Morgan etch #1428 Orchid Tints pitcher, $2500-3000.

Morgan etch #67 compotes, 6" tall, 5" top, $350-425; 6" tall, 6" top, $750-800.

Morgan etch #1428 Orchid Tints water goblet, $200-275.

Morgan etch #43, 6 oz. tumbler in rose color, $175-200.

Morgan etch #1447, 10 oz. water tumbler, blue, $225-250.

Morgan etch #780, 6 oz. saucer champagne, dual plate etched, with rayed base and monogrammed, etched "M", for Governor Morgan, unable to price due to scarcity.

Morgan etch #1428 saucer champagne, in Orchid Tints, $200-210.

Morgan etch #1428 wine in Orchid Tints, $225-275.

Morgan etch #1435 pastry tray, or center handled servers, in rose color, $275-300.

Morgan etch, unknown line number, "baseball bat stem" saucer champagne in amber, $110-125.

Morgan etch #1450 water tumbler, in crystal, $225, and sherbet, $200.

Morgan etch #2005 bon-bons (or what happens to a cream soup if you pull the sides down when hot), in amber, $75-90; and rose colors, $150-195.

Morgan etch footed whipped cream bowl in amber, $275.

Morgan etch footed whipped cream dish in rose $375.

Morgan etch #1470, fruit salad bowls in crystal, $145; in rose, $225.

Morgan etch #2000 candles in blue, $2200 pair; and #2000 center piece bowl in blue, $900.

Morgan etch water goblet, 8-5/16" tall, 3-11/16" top, blue/crystal, $225-275; blue luncheon plate, $75-90.

Morgan etch #1426 saucer champagne in rose color, $125.

Morgan etch #2000, 12" octagon console bowl in rose color, $325.

Morgan etch saucer champagne, 5-15/16" tall, 3-15/16" top, in rose color, $175.

Morgan etch 4 oz. cocktail, 5-5/8" tall, 2-3/4" top, $195.

Morgan etch #818 water goblet in rose, $175.

Morgan etch #1440 water goblet, $250-275.

Morgan etch #1445, 12 oz. water tumbler in rose, $225.

Morgan etch 2002 footed mayo/liner/ladle, $325.

Morgan etch octagon candles, $325 pair.

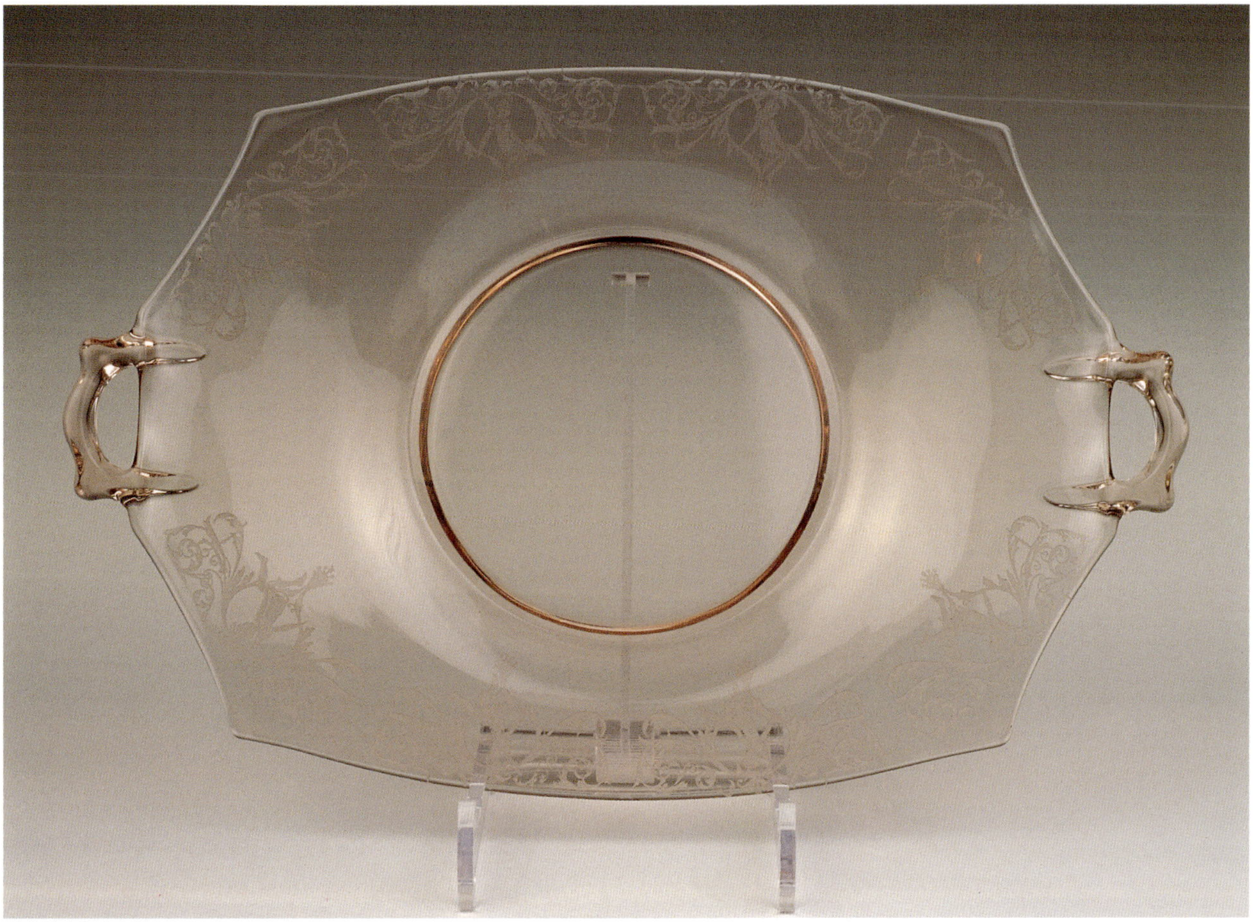

Morgan etch #2002, 15" platter in rose, $275.

Morgan etch #2001 mayo and spoon in green with red/gold highlights, $425.

Morgan etch #2001, 12" rolled edge console bowl in rose color, $250.

Morgan etch #530, 12 oz. St. Regis water tumbler, crystal with dual plate etch, $195-200.

Morgan etch crystal oyster cocktail, 3-1/2" tall, 3-3/8" top, $95-110.

Morgan etch saucer champagne in crystal, 5-15/16" tall, 3-15/16" top, $125.

Morgan etch #818 crystal water goblet, $135; and sherbet, $110.

Morgan etch #1447 tall water tumbler in crystal, $105-115.

Morgan etch #2005 cup and saucer, $250-300.

Morgan etch sugar, $175-200.

Morgan etch saucer champagnes in blue/crystal, bead stem and single wafer disc separator, $150-175.

Morgan etch crystal/green, tall water goblet, $150; saucer champagne, $125; wine, $150.

Morgan etch dinner plate in Orchid Tints, unable to price due to scarcity.

Morgan etch ice tub in rose color, $600-750; rectangle in crystal, $995-1200.

# Etch #421 Veninga

## Colors: green, rose, combinations of color and crystal

Etch #421 as the company knew it would later gain its name from Hazel Marie Weatherman in the book all glass collectors call "the bible," *Colored Glassware of the Depression Era Book Two*. While only two pages are shown with Central Glass Works information, they were very important to all of the folks seeking information on this company. Although there are only two pages of CGW's items in that area, we found we could see many of the items Central Glass produced in the Lotus section of that book. At least 75% of the wares Lotus decorated at this time were CGW's blanks. Also, a quick trip to the Monongah section of the same book shows many Central blanks there as well. The bottom of page 275 will be all CGW's blanks.

The Veninga etch is very elaborate, beautifully designed, and belongs in a category with all of the well designed etches of the period. The problem again is finding examples to fill a few place settings. To date, all I have seen are stems and some serving pieces. Although the catalogs would have us believe there are only stems, tumblers, and a fruit salad bowl to be found, it has also been found on items like the 2001 fruit basket. Ten pieces are shown in the catalog; five stems, four tumblers, and the small-footed bowl. I also have examples on the beaded, graduated ball stem. Now we need to go find more. Catalog copy in the #1447 line number section will show a very good example of the etching.

| Item | size or line | all color combinations |
|---|---|---|
| Bowl fruit salad footed | #1447 | |
| Bowl handled basket | #2001 | $35 |
| Cocktail | #1447 | |
| Saucer champagne | #1447 6 oz. | $40-45 |
| Sherbet | #1447 6 oz. | $35-40 |
| Wine | #1447 | |
| Goblet water | #1447 10 oz. | $175-195 |
| Saucer champagne | bead stem | $35-40 |
| Water goblet | bead stem | $35-40 |
| Tumbler | #1447 2-3/4 oz. | |
| Tumbler | #1447 7 oz. | |
| Tumbler | #1447 10 oz. | $20-25 |
| Tumbler | #1447 12 oz. | $30 |

Veninga #1447, 10 oz. tumbler, crystal $25-30; bead stem saucer champagne, crystal, $30-35.

Veninga #1447 walnut stem saucer champagne, green/crystal, $40-45.

Veninga 7-1/2" salad plate, green, $25-30.

## Etch #425 Wheeling Floral

### Colors: rose, green, and combinations of crystal with rose and green

The upper part of this etch looks like a big smile filled with flowers, while the lower potion of the etch looks like a cameo filled with flowers. While most patterns by CGW during this time will show stems and tumblers, this pattern also shows plates in sizes 6 to 10-inch, with only the rose color being produced. Catalog items shown are stems, cocktail, saucer champagne, sherbet, wine, parfait, and water goblet, tumblers: 2 3/4 oz. grape juice, 7 oz. orange juice, 10 oz. water, and 12 oz. water. Plates in the #1384-1/2 line are only shown in rose color, sizes are 6-1/2-inches for the bread plate all the way up to 9-1/2-inches for a small dinner, and the 10-inch dinner plate.

## Etch #422 Bordered Urns & Medallions

### Colors: rose, green, & combinations of crystal with rose or green

While there are again eleven items shown in the catalog, I have not seen one piece to acquire. Stems, tumblers, and a fruit salad bowl make up the catalog line, but like other similar patterns, there should be more found. Look in the #1445 line numbers section for the catalog copy showing the #422 etch. Pieces you will find are: the footed fruit salad; stems: cocktail, sherbet, saucer champagne, wine, water goblet, Parfait; tumblers: 2-3/4 oz. grape juice, 7 oz. orange juice, 10 oz. water, and the 12 oz. water.

Etch #425 Wheeling Floral 8-1/2" luncheon plate in crystal, $15.

# Etch #430 Kay

### Crystal, rose, amber, and green, combinations of crystal, and colors

The etch will be found on the 1451 tumbler line, the 1448 stem and tumbler line, and #1450 plates. This has the potential to be a large set if we can get it out of hiding. Pieces in the catalog are shown below. Because the etch will be found on the 1451 and 1450 lines, I would expect to find many more pieces than are listed here. Pieces like creamers and sugars, celery dishes, and just about anything found on the above mentioned lines should be discovered. Below are items that are listed in the catalog, but I have never seen them to gather prices.

| Item | line | size |
|---|---|---|
| Bowl | #1448 | Fruit |
| Cocktail | #1448 | 3 oz. |
| Saucer champagne | #1448 | 6 oz. |
| Sherbet | #1448 | 6 oz. |
| Wine | #1448 | 3 oz. |
| Water goblet | #1448 | 10 oz. |
| Tumbler | #1448 | 2-3/4 grape juice |
| Tumbler | #1448 | oyster cocktail |
| Tumbler | #1448 | 5 oz. orange juice |
| Tumbler | #1448 | 8 oz. water |
| Tumbler | #1448 | 10 oz. |
| Tumbler | #1448 | 12 oz. |
| Cocktail | #1451 | 3 oz. |
| Sherbet | #1451 | 5-1/2 oz. |
| Wine | #1451 | 3 oz. |
| Goblet | #1451 | 9 oz. |
| Plate | #1450 | 6" |
| Plate | #1450 | 7" |
| Plate | #1450 | 8" |
| Plate | #1450 | 9" |

Etch #430 Kay, on the #1451 line sherbet in amber, $35-40.

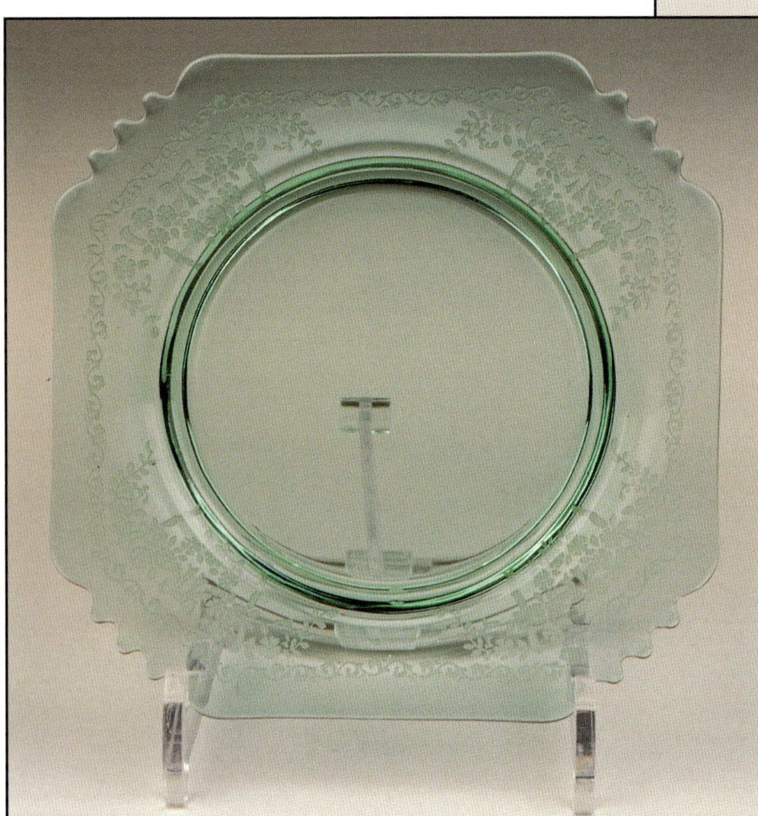

Etch #430 Kay, on the #1450 line, 6-9/16" bread and butter plate, in green, $20-25.

# Etch #431 Deco

### Colors: crystal with Orchid Tints, rose, green, black, and amber

Truly a "deco in design" etching, this pattern has only been found on the numbers 1450 and 1451 lines, which it seems best suited for anyway. Shown are the large fruit salad bowl and a sherbet. Like other patterns found on the blanks, 1450 & 1451, much more of this etch should be found.

Etch #431 Deco, #1450 sherbet in crystal and rose, $45.

Etch #431 Deco, #1450 fruit salad bowl in crystal and Orchid Tints, $75-90.

Etch #431 fruit salad and sherbets shown side by side for comparison.

# Etch #432 Hester

## Colors: crystal, Golden Sapphire & crystal (rose in green shown in catalog), may be found in ebony

The Hester, or #432 etch, appears to be lower in popularity to the more well known sister pattern, Morgan. This I believe is due to the fact that Morgan is not only collected by Elegant Glass aficionados, but also by those interested in collecting items with fairies or angels. If at all possible, it seems this etch is even more difficult to locate than the more popular Central patterns. Pieces in this pattern are almost non-existent and should not be passed up when found in any color or shape.

An Internet auction purchase in December of 2002 netted a #904, cut 7, 5-1/2 oz. sham (whisky on the rocks) tumbler in crystal. This bar sized tumbler (in my mind) would prove to us the existence of a whisky decanter set in this line. If the piece had not been etched, I would believe it to be part of the line sold to and used by establishments that served alcohol during the 1920s and '30s. However, the fact that this little gem is etched with the #432 Hester pattern gives me the belief that we will find an etched decanter with a set of these glasses soon.

While the catalog shows and claims this etch was also produced in rose and green on the #1470 line of stems, I haven't seen any. Nor have I seen any green or rose 1470 stems free of etching. I would be very excited to see either. Another find in 2002 was the discovery of #432, etched on the #1448 line of stems. Previously to 2002 Hester was only found by collectors on the #1470 line of stems, and the #1450 dinnerware. The excitement continues to grow for this obscure etch, and it should be considered that we will (or should) find this etch on more lines produced by CGW.

Something else worth noting is that the saucer has a perched or raised cup ring that just fits the base of the cup, although the ring is round, and the base of the cup square. The edges of the saucers are also curved up slightly coming away from the center of the saucer. Also, the sherbet liner plate has a ring for the base of the rounded sherbet though this area is not raised like the saucer. The regular plates in this size do not have these features.

| Item | Line number | crystal | crystal/ golden sapphire |
|---|---|---|---|
| Bowl fruit salad | #1470 | | |
| Bowl cereal | #2019 | | $135 |
| Bowl grapefruit | #1450 | | |
| Bowl celery | #1450 | | |
| Bowl mayonnaise | #2002 | | $125 |
| Bowl pickle | #1450 | | |
| Bowl relish | #1450 | | |
| Bowl vegetable | #1450 | | |
| Bowl bon-bon | #2019 | | $75-90 |
| Comport | #1470 | $195 | $375 |
| Creamer | #1450 | $65 | $95 |
| Creamer | #deco fan & plume | $75 | |
| Cup/Saucer | #1450 | $75 | $150-175 |
| Plate bread & butter | #1450 | | $25 |
| Plate 7" salad | #1450 | | $45 |
| Plate 8" lunch | #1450 | | $95 |
| Plate 9" dinner | #1450 | | $125 |
| Stem champagne | #1470 | $45 | $75 |
| Stem cocktail | | $45 | $75 |
| Stem cordial | | $50 | $75 |
| Stem goblet water | | $75 | $95 |
| Stem parfait | | $75 | $95 |
| Stem wine | | $75 | $95 |
| Stem sherbet | | $45 | $85-95 |
| Tumbler oyster cocktail | #1470 | $50 | $95-125 |
| Tumbler 2-3/4 oz. grape | #1470 | | |
| Tumbler 10 oz. water | #1470 | | |
| Tumbler 12 oz. water | #1470 | | |
| Tray pastry | #1450 | | |

Etch #432 Hester catalog copy. *Courtesy Dean Six.*

Etch #432 Hester #1448 wine in crystal, $225-250.

Etch #432 Hester #1470 compote in Golden Sapphire/Crystal, $375.

Etch #432 Hester #2019 bon-bon in Golden Sapphire, $75-90.

Etch #432 Hester #1470 oyster cocktail in golden Sapphire/Crystal, $95-125.

Etch #432 Hester #1470 sherbet in Golden Sapphire/Crystal, $85-95.

Etch #432 Hester #1470 sherbet in crystal, $45.

Etch #432 Hester #2002 mayo in crystal, $145.

Etch #432 Hester Deco Fan creamer and sugar in crystal, $150-175.

Etch #432 Hester #1470 sherbet with #1450 liner in Golden Sapphire, $125-135.

Etch #432 Hester #1450 cup and saucer in Golden Sapphire, $150-175.

Etch #432 Hester #1470 cocktail, in crystal, $45.

Etch #432 Hester 4 oz. whiskey sham, 3-1/8" tall, 2-1/4" top, crystal, $95.

Etch #432 Hester #1450 plates in Golden Sapphire, 8-1/2", $125; 7-1/2", $95.

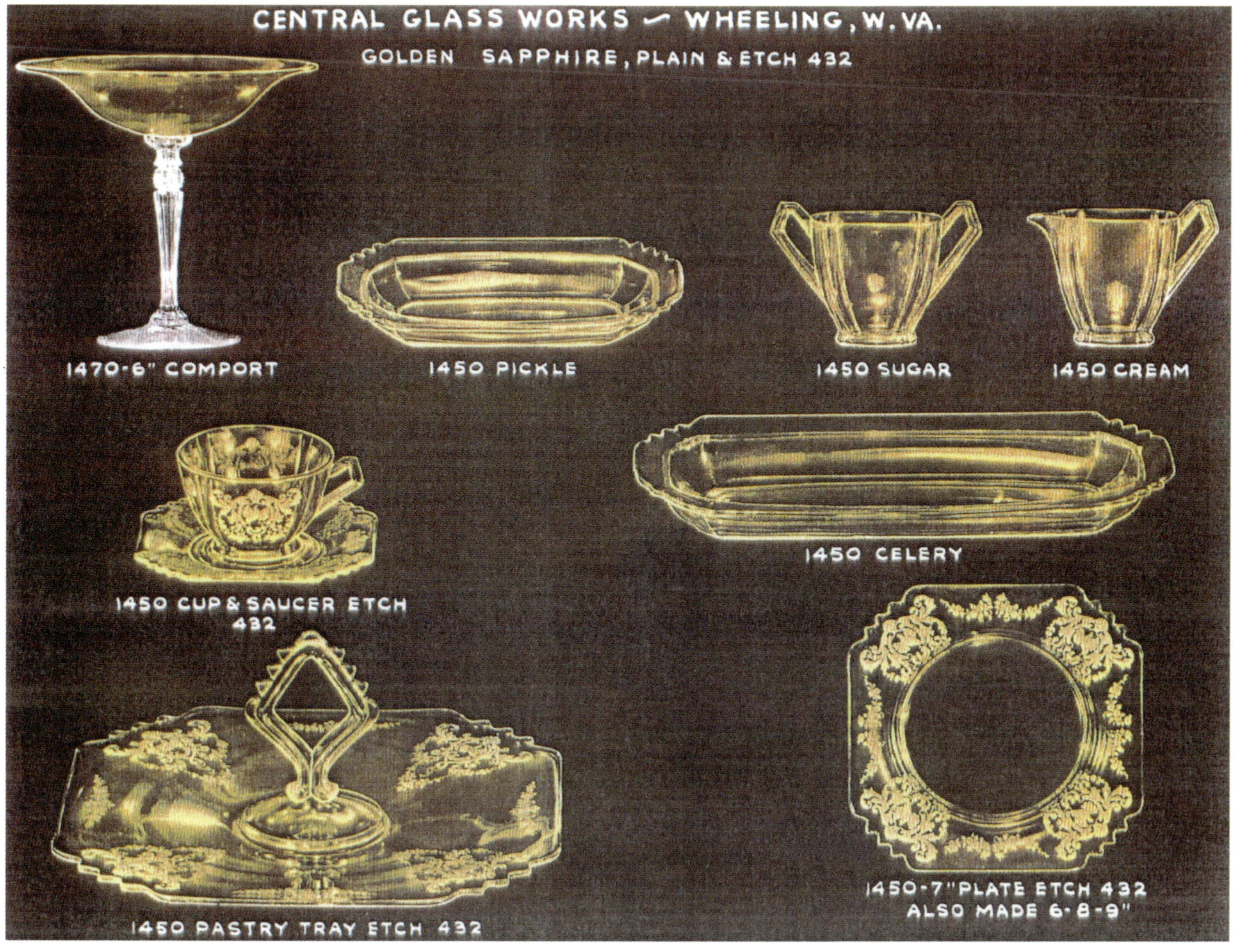


Etch #432 Hester. *Catalog copy courtesy Dean Six .*

# Decoration #280

### Hand-painted florals

A simple hand-painted floral decoration from the catalogs called #280. The only place I have found it is on serving pieces like the centered handled servers, etc.

Decoration #280, hand painted floral decorations or decals on pastry tray, $25-30.

## 19$^{th}$ Hole

### Hand-painted on stemware

I have looked for these stems for years, and when I finally did find them, was not able to pay more than the golfers who also would go after them. These simple stems have sold for well over $100 each in quantities. Now, golfers don't care that they're old; they just buy them because they're golf-related. They don't know that Central Glass made them in the early 1930s; it's just golf stuff. A few different styles of golfers, hand-painted in enamel on the #1470 blanks, in period clothing, will be found. Sorry, no photos to share. Expect to pay between $100 and $200 dollars for each stem.

## Stretch Glass by Central

Central trumpet shape, Stretch candlesticks in cobalt blue, *Courtesy Jan Reichling,* $125-150.

Central Glass Works did produce Stretch Glass during the depression era, and it is as well made as all the companies much more famous for their productions of these wares. Central Stretch is scarce at best, and cobalt stretch almost non-existent. Either it was not heavily made or is already in collections. Thanks to Jan Reichling for sharing her collection.

Central trumpet Stretch candlesticks in green, *Courtesy Jan Reichling,* $75-100.

## Art Glass by Central

I guess the most widely seen forms of Art Glass by this company would be the opal bowls and serving pieces. The opal lines will be sold or marketed most often as products made by the Fry Glass Company and are identical in most respects. The Central items I have seen have all been iridized as well. While the crystal/opal combinations are most common, items in colors like the console set of amethyst/opal and the compote in green/opal are extremely rare and impossible to price. These items were expensive when they sold during the 1920s and '30s, and today are basically untouchable to common collectors like me. Candlesticks were advertised by Central in sizes as tall as 17-inches. Enjoy the photos of these rarities. Many thanks to Neil and Ethel (Eddie) Unger for sharing their collection.

Central console set with footed bowl and large trumpet candlesticks in blue, *Courtesy Jan Reichling*, $225-250.

Central Glass Works Art Glass console set, amethyst and opal, *Courtesy Neil and Ethel Unger*, unable to price due to scarcity.

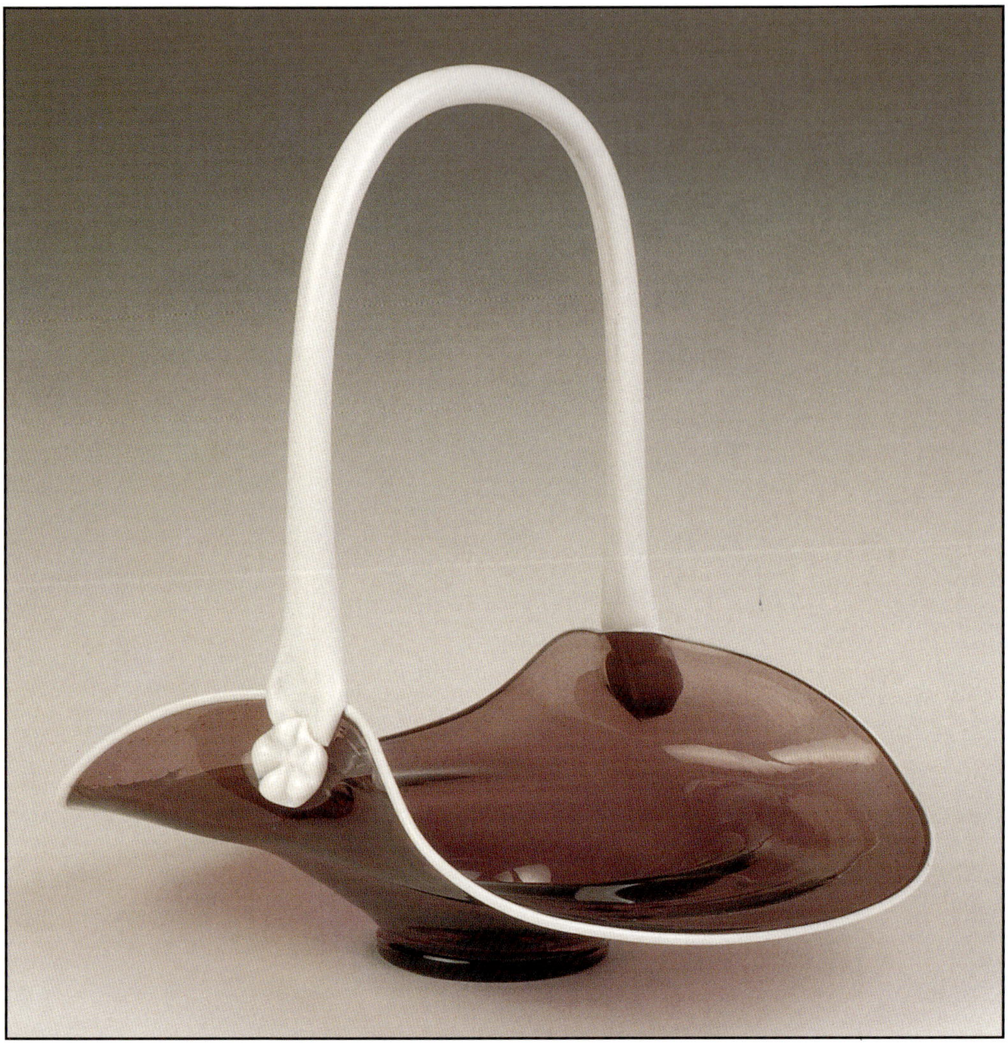

Central Glass Works amethyst and opal basket, *Courtesy Neil and Ethel Unger,* unable to price due to scarcity.

Central Glass Works, Art Glass opal iridized bowl, $75-90.

# Unknown Etchings

## Colors vary by items

What I would like to add here is a bit about items etched by Central Glass Works, which I cannot find to this point in company catalogs, yet the etch does not appear in catalogs by other companies that were still around long after CGW was out of business, such as Lotus Decorating. Attribution could be by trade journal or deductive logic. So, until we know them not to be Central, we will list them here, and/or change them to correct etch numbers or names as we find out more.

## American Beauty

### 1938 release in crystal and unknown if any produced in color

This etched bowl and platter appeared in *Crockery and Glass Journal* 1938 in an ad titled "Right Out Of The Kiln."

> American Beauty Line from Central Glass Co. is shown by Frances H. Ruhe, Inc., includes sixteen decorative pieces richly gold-decorated and moderately priced.

This is a wealth of information from a company about to take its last breath. While I have never seen a piece of this in person, I wonder how much made it out into the publics' hands before Imperial started distribution of this blank with etches like the Belmont Hills Cutting.

As in many later references, Central again refers to itself as Central Glass Company in this trade journal release, hoping to draw from their successful, established past history.

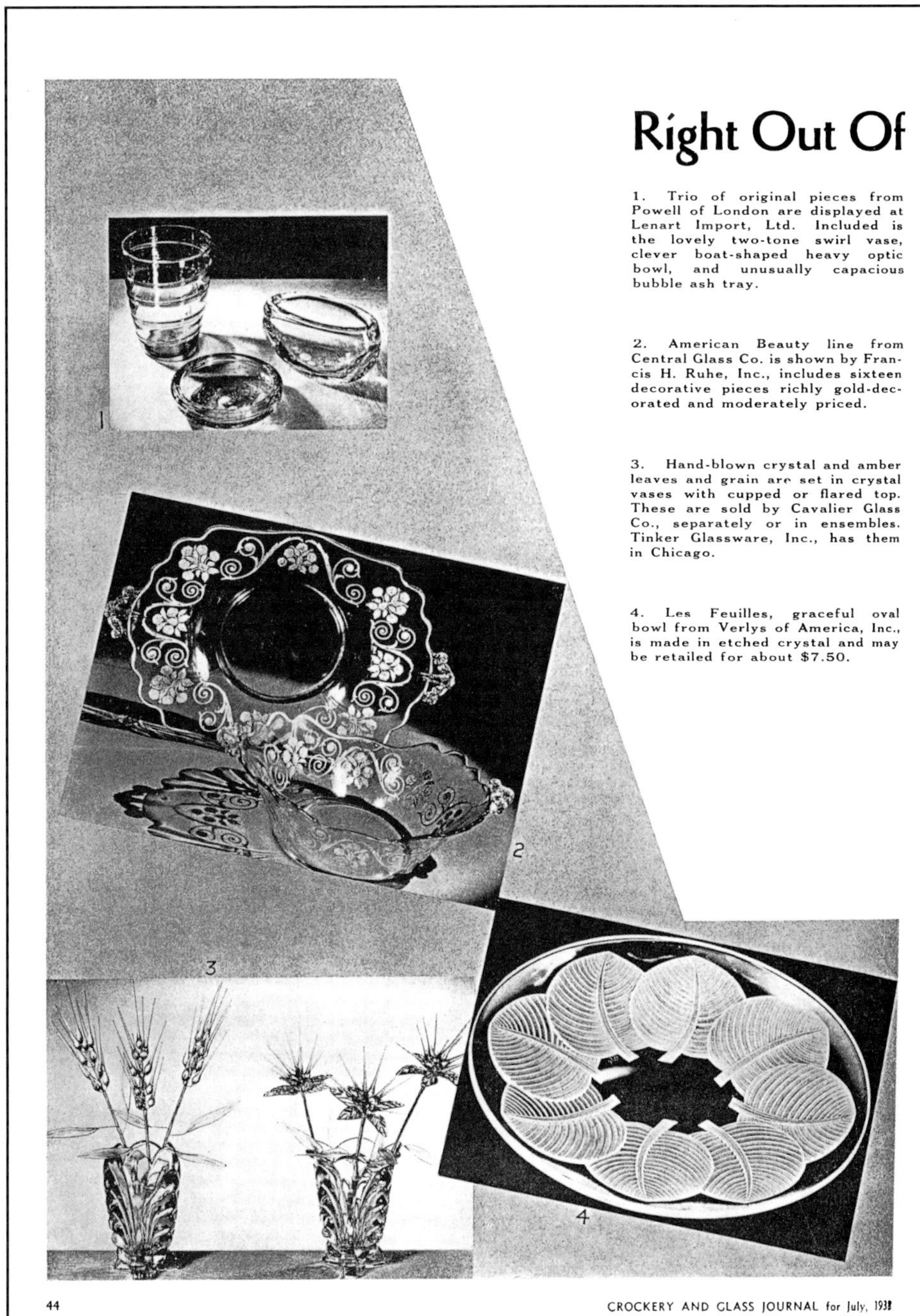

Right Out Of

1. Trio of original pieces from Powell of London are displayed at Lenart Import, Ltd. Included is the lovely two-tone swirl vase, clever boat-shaped heavy optic bowl, and unusually capacious bubble ash tray.

2. American Beauty line from Central Glass Co. is shown by Francis H. Ruhe, Inc., includes sixteen decorative pieces richly gold-decorated and moderately priced.

3. Hand-blown crystal and amber leaves and grain are set in crystal vases with cupped or flared top. These are sold by Cavalier Glass Co., separately or in ensembles. Tinker Glassware, Inc., has them in Chicago.

4. Les Feuilles, graceful oval bowl from Verlys of America, Inc., is made in etched crystal and may be retailed for about $7.50.

44 CROCKERY AND GLASS JOURNAL for July, 1938

Trade journal copy of the American Beauty line, July 1938.

# Aster (chrysanthemum)

### Colors: rose found but should be green and amber also

I have three pieces of this etch I bought as an example because they were all on Central Glass blanks. While I have not verified this etch in a catalog, it looks very similar to Tiffin's Aster. It may have been some of that shareware, although I believe the mum flower rises in the Tiffin example, where here with the CGW flower it hangs downward. The blanks are CGW all the way though. Included is a bottom view of a CGW plate and a couple of close-ups. The shape of their plates is like that of no other company.

Aster etch close-up on lunch plate.

View of the underside of the Central plate showing how deep the centers are.

Aster lunch plate in rose, $15-20; Aster etched #1445, 10 oz. tumbler in rose, $18-20; Aster etched saucer champagne in rose, $15-18.

Aster etch close-up on tumbler.

Dunn's Parrot etching on #1422 cigarette holder, $150-195.

Dunn's Parrot etching, on #1320/168, 10" bud vase in amber with original sticker, $175.

# Dunn's Parrot

### Colors: amber, rose, green, crystal, and colors with gold fill

How does one justify this being a CGW etch if I have not personally found it in a catalog by Central? I have an amber vase with the gold-filled Parrot etch, with an original Central Glass Works sticker. Dunn's Parrot etch will be found on many different lines by Central. At first this etching was only found on vases and odd assorted serving pieces like cigarette holders. Recently a crystal tumbler was discovered, so I'm sure we will find many more table service items, although scarce, in the future. All the pieces below except the tumbler are priced with gold filled etch.

| Item | crystal | colors | black |
|---|---|---|---|
| Fan vase | | $95-125 | $195-225 |
| Bud vase | | $95-125 | $125-150 |
| Cig. holder | | $150-195 | |
| Tumbler 10 oz. | $45 | | |

# Grigg's Etch

Grigg's etch on #1470 stems in crystal, each $35-40.

## Crystal

The pattern, Grigg's etch, is without a doubt one of the missing Central Glass Works patterns. Typical in design of so many other examples of Central's products, finding it etched on the #1470 stem lines is a real treat. Below you will find a close-up of this etch, along with an etched water goblet and saucer champagne.

Grigg's etch close-up.

# Havana, Larieux, & Leonardo Cuttings

## Crystal

Central released new hand cuttings by very talented craftsman in 1938 just before going out of business. In an attempt to revive slow sales in a very tough market, they released some beautiful stemware during this time. Shown in the trade journal release are the cutting patterns Havana, Larieux, and Leonardo. These wares were a bold and different attempt for Central Glass Works. The crystal was of the highest quality, and the cuttings by the best craftsman in the business.

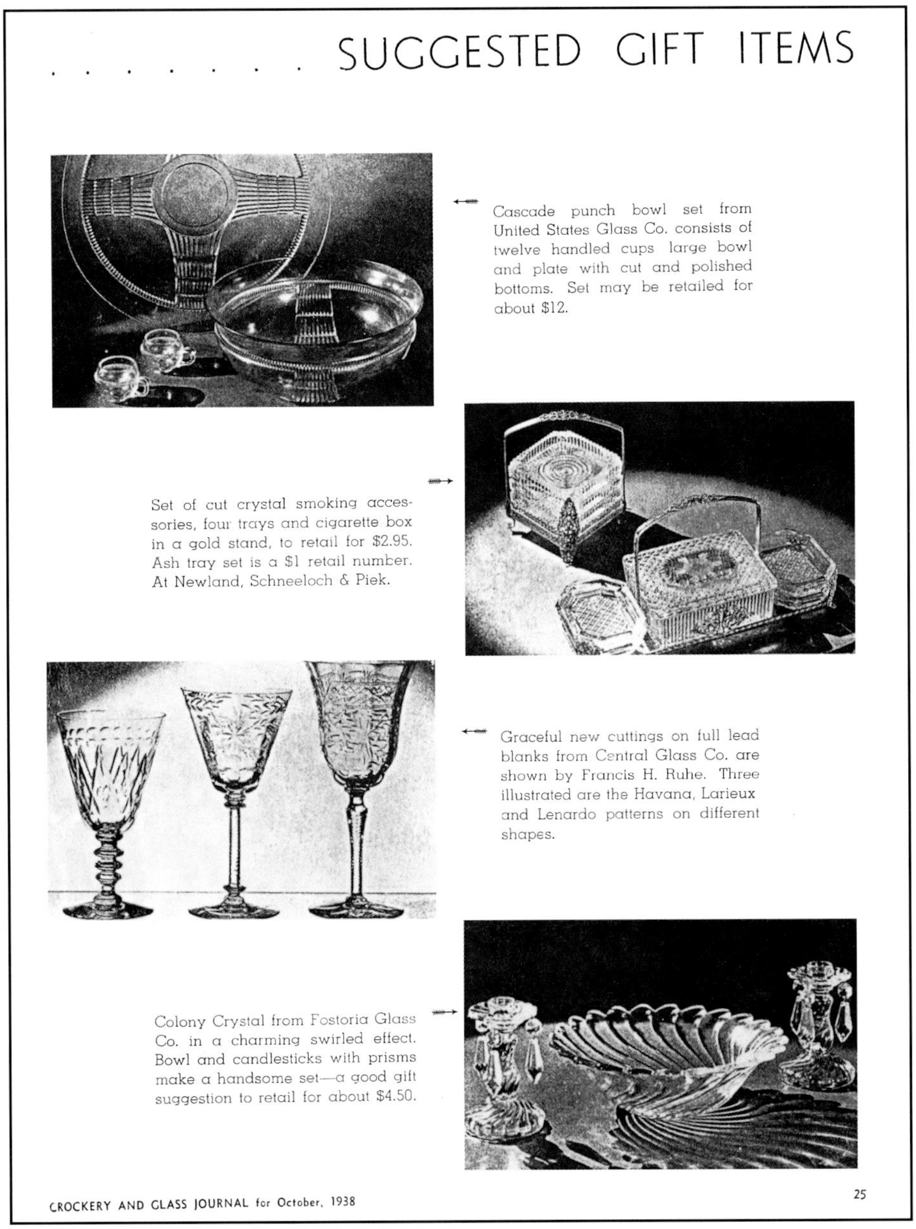

. . . . . . . . SUGGESTED GIFT ITEMS

Cascade punch bowl set from United States Glass Co. consists of twelve handled cups large bowl and plate with cut and polished bottoms. Set may be retailed for about $12.

Set of cut crystal smoking accessories, four trays and cigarette box in a gold stand, to retail for $2.95. Ash tray set is a $1 retail number. At Newland, Schneeloch & Piek.

Graceful new cuttings on full lead blanks from Central Glass Co. are shown by Francis H. Ruhe. Three illustrated are the Havana, Larieux and Lenardo patterns on different shapes.

Colony Crystal from Fostoria Glass Co. in a charming swirled effect. Bowl and candlesticks with prisms make a handsome set—a good gift suggestion to retail for about $4.50.

CROCKERY AND GLASS JOURNAL for October, 1938 — 25

Trade journal page showing new releases of hand cuttings Havana, Larieux, & Leonardo.

# Roses & Bows

The Roses & Bows etch, while not appearing in a catalog that I have seen, does come to us from a trade journal article showing us it was manufactured by Central just before 1920. It has been found so far only in crystal and only in stem lines.

Wm. F. Hayes & Co., silver-deposit ware, represented by Wm. H. Richter; the W. & S. Mfg. Co., silver-plated and glass novelties; and B. J. De Passe, Inc., silver-deposit ware, represented by R. E. Leyendecker, Inc.—share the quarters. The fact that three birds may be killed with one stone will be appreciated by buyers who are rushed for time.

ATTRACTIVE STEMWARE.

The accompanying illustration shows one of the Central Glass Works' newest designs. The gracefulness of the deep plate etching and the refined simplicity of the well-proportioned shape have met with unqualified approval. It is made in a complete line of stemware, which may be seen, together with many other attractive patterns, at the concern's New York showroom, 1107 Broadway, in charge of A. P. Doctor.

EFFECTIVE DINNERWARE DECORATION.

One of the newest achievements in artistic open stock dinnerware designs turned out by John Maddock & Sons, now on view at the showroom of Maddock & Miller, is the "Tokio" pattern, which, as the name implies, is Japanese in character, yet entirely different from the designs ordinarily seen in this style. An attractive feature is a light French gray background in

Roses and Bows advertisement, *Crockery & Glass Journal.*

Roses and Bows etch on #112 water goblet, $12-15.

# Silhouette

## Silver overlay on various blanks

The Silhouette pattern is simply a treatment found only on CGW patterns or blanks and consists of a female head silhouette, floral decorations, and urns filled with flowers. I have seen this pattern on bowls and other serving pieces by CGW, but never on any other glass manufacturers' products. Treatments have been found on candlesticks and matching console bowls and even decorated pieces of the Frances (2010) line. This may have been a special order for one particular client and covered many lines by CGW. Pieces will not be terribly expensive as there is no complete set to be had.

Silhouette silver plate decoration close-up.

# Candlesticks & Holders

Central Glass Works made many different kinds of candlesticks as you have seen in the previous chapters of this reference. The line numbers are unknown for the candlesticks shown in the following images, but the short, rose-colored Georgian mushroom-shaped candles are on the cover of the Central Glass catalog shot that reads "New Beauty in Glass from Old Central." I wanted to show these sticks from both views, so one is upside down.

Georgian (unknown line number) candlesticks in rose color, $75-80 pair.

**Opposite page, top:**
Vaseline trumpet candlestick, $55-60; cobalt trumpet candlestick, $45-55.

**Opposite page, bottom:**
Miscellaneous tall trumpet candlesticks, $10-20 each.

# Earlier Items by Central Glass Works

## Colors: crystal, Vaseline, amber

Shown following this article are items produced by Central before the depression era. I personally have found the Thumbprint and Lattice sugar jar with a Fenton logo, so it was reproduced at one point. The folks at Fenton tell me that because the piece does not carry the scripted F in the logo that it is their own mold. If it were another company's mold, the Fenton logo **would** start with the scripted **F**. The color of the pieces I have seen was way off for CGW's works, some in a beautiful dichromatic color. As promised, I would add items that were pre-depression if they had been reproduced, or were just too neat to leave out. So you get some of the Thumbprint and Lattice items and some nice old lamps. Remember, to see more of Central Glass Company's work, you will have to grab a copy of *Central Glass Company, The First Thirty Years*, a Schiffer Publication.

Central Glass Works Thumbprint & Lattice creamer in Electric Blue, $125; covered butter in Canary Yellow, $325; muffineer in Canary Yellow, $275.

Central Glass #983 decanters, Penwick Rye and Alett Special Reserve, $60-90.

Central Glass beer barrel tumbler #925, 9 oz., $35-50.

Central Glass hand painted oil lamp cabin scene, $375-400.

Central Glass lamp, $175-225.

# Look-A-Like Patterns or Etchings

What follows are descriptions of items made by other companies that copied items made by Central Glass Works. This does not mean that Central made them first; this is just a glimpse or description of those look-a-like items. Images will follow at the end of descriptions.

## #402 Etch

Central and Heisey both made this etch, but the Heisey Zodiac etching has an extra cord tassel hanging from the center of the medallion not found on CGW lines. Other than the cord tassel, there are minor differences in the urn at the top of the etched area between the bands.

## #983 Decanters

Central never made these decanters in anything but crystal. Although similar in design from the shape of the vessel to the stoppers, those colored items were made in Weston, West Virginia, by Louie, and by New Martinsville glass companies.

## #1450 Line

I would like to explain the differences in the 1450 line of plates and serving pieces. The CGW 1450 has pronounced peaks in the corners, and straight lateral lines between the corners. New Martinsville has a similar line that has peaks in the corners but has more little bumps on their straight or lateral edges between the corners. Their pattern was/is called #36. (Weatherman's *Book Two* page 299, top left.)

Fostoria's Mayfair pattern has rolling scallops on their corners, more like gentle rolling hills with no small beads or bumps on the straight edges between the corners.

The 1450 line by CGW also shares a look-a-like in the creamer and sugar department. Central's creamer and sugar has a light and delicate look with better lines in a deco fashion. The four corners of the body on the blank curve inward to the center. The base is square, but where the corners extend to the base, the glass folds in and basically leaves a void in the four corners of the base. The look-a-like pieces were made by Paden City, and are part of the Mrs. B line. They are more bulky, and the four corners are rounded to the outside and the base is more round than square.

## #1426 Cord Stem

Just a note on this line: it will also be found in the Tiffin and Bryce glass company catalogs. Telling the blanks apart without a known etch is impossible except for small differences in color. Keep in mind that the CGW rose color has more purple than Tiffin, and will aid in color matching the company's wares.

## #1428 Decanter

The deco or #1428 decanters will be a bit more of a challenge, telling the differences between companies apart. Most of the better glass companies made this style of decanter. You will find representative styles by Cambridge and Paden City to be the closest to Central's. Remember, Central's stoppers will be very valuable in the times ahead, as collectors looking for these pieces for their popular etched decanters will be taking them from examples without etching.

## Harding (Griffins)

The next look-a-like is Eldorado by Tiffin. This one is not too hard. If the griffins face each other and have their heads raised with tongues out lapping water from an urn, and are seated on their hind legs, that's Harding by Central Glass Works. If the griffins are back to back, that is Eldorado by Tiffin Glass Company. If the figures are facing each other and they look more like lions and the etch is very poorly done, that's New Martinsville's Lions pattern.

## Grape etch #6

On the Grape etch by Central, look for the close-up of the cursive E in the pattern. Also, to the right of that cursive E, that bunch of grapes is held on to the vine by what looks like two little wire ornament hangers. If it is not this way, it's not CGW's etch #6 Grape. Fry, Morgantown, Fostoria, and most of the companies made a similar etch. Some companies made more than one.

## #2019 Line bowls & serving pieces

This line is usually confused with Cambridge lines due to handle similarities. A basic, quick way to tell CGW handles from Cambridge is to put two normal sized fingers into the handle. The Central handle is larger, almost looking like an old bottle opener, where the Cambridge handle opening is smaller and would probably allow the passing of maybe one finger through the handle. See the close-ups.

Now the real problem is telling the difference between Central's 2019 line and New Martinsville's 2019 line. Why? Because the two lines are exactly the same product. Identical. So who owned the molds and who bought from whom? In talking with New Martinsville collectors, it would appear that color *will* make a difference in undecorated blanks. Since I have the blank etched with the Hester pattern in Golden Sapphire, and the Morgan etch in ebony, there is no doubt in my mind who made the blank. Reference for the New Martinsville #2019 line, *Weatherman's Colored Glassware of the Depression Era, Book Two*, page 299 top of page.

## Rose Etch #23

Check the close-up of the CGW Rose etch 23 pattern and remember it will be found with a dual plate etching at times. There are many rose etchings out there, so remember the details in the pattern. This is most often confused with the works of Fry Glass Company. See the enhanced pattern shot in the etch #23 section.

Central Glass Works #1428 decanter in green and the look-a-like in lavender.

Heisey Zodiac tumbler, etching almost exactly matches Central's #402 etch.

Central glass #983 decanter in crystal and the look-a-like made by both Louie and New Martinsville in blue.

Bottom and inside view of CGW's #1450 sugar and creamer shapes.

Paden City Mrs. B creamer and sugar, look-a-likes of Central's #1450 line, $30-45 set.

Heisey tumbler in the Renaissance pattern, same designer as the Morgan etch, $35-40.

A look-a-like pattern by Tiffin that resembles many Central Glass patterns including an almost exact match for the David pattern, tumbler $10-15.

This bowl found etched by Paden City (Cupid pattern), and Central Glass Works (Morgan pattern), in not etched, $15-18.

Central Glass Works #1450 sugar in rose color, and the Paden City Mrs. B sugar in yellow.

New Martinsville's #36 divided relish, look-a-like of Central's #1450 line, *Courtesy of Rod Moore,* $65-75.

**Right and below:** Close-up of Central handles #2019 line bon-bon.

Close-up of the Cambridge look-a-like handles.

Close-up of Fostoria Mayfair plate showing corner differences.

Grape etch close-up, closely matching Central Glass Works, unknown maker.

# Imperial Glass Company Reissues of Central Glass Works Items

When Imperial acquired the equipment of Central Glass Works around 1940, they reissued **many** of the lines in stemware and serving pieces. Stemware such as the beautiful #1470 line was reproduced with some of Imperial's own etchings, like the fabulous Butterfly etching and patterns like Garden Arbor. When Imperial reissued this line, it appears to me that they added more glass to the lip area of the glass, making it a bit more durable than CGW had. Imperial also produced the stemware without an etch in some of their own colors like a smoke color and a darker color that actually changed into different shades of blue, smoke, and purple depending on what type of light was cast on the stem.

Imperial reissued those big handled serving pieces with etches or cuttings like Belmont Hills. They will also have redone the line of candlesticks and bowls in the Deco Fan line in plain crystal and with their own cuttings.

Imperial would also show in their catalogs Central's cheese and cracker tray, center handled server, and mayo dish, in their own colors.

Imperial's Butterfly etch on Central's #1470 stemmed water goblet, $75-90.

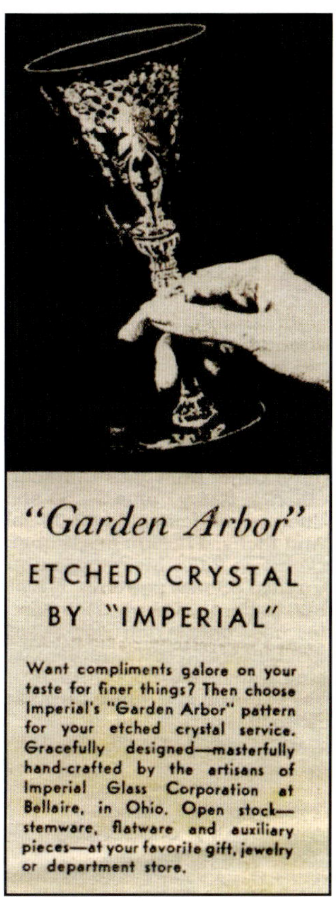


Imperial's Garden Arbor ad, copy from *Unknown source* .

# Central's Barware

I know you're thinking that since Central Glass Works (Company) was always known primarily as a barware glass maker, that this chapter will be pages and pages of the stuff they made during their lifetime. This isn't so. What will be shown are the trade journal copies of some of the depression era items they produced, and some of the more popularly found stems, long attributed to other companies.

CROCKERY AND GLASS JOURNAL
1170 Broadway, New York, N. Y.

Gentlemen: Enclosed please find list of names. Please send subscriptions to us at the SPECIAL GROUP RATE mentioned below.

☐ Here is a check for $..........

☐ Bill us later.

USE
THE
COUPON ABOVE
AND
SAVE
50%

BUYERS!
STORE OWNERS!
DEPARTMENT MANAGERS!

Have you ever thought how helpful CROCKERY AND GLASS JOURNAL would be to your assistants?

All alert executives or assistants under you should take advantage of every opportunity to enrich his store of style, merchandising and selling ideas.

CROCKERY AND GLASS JOURNAL is a regular business-building conference each month, and can be a source of inspiration and guidance to everyone in the industry.

SPECIAL GROUP RATE
(for the U. S. only)

3 or more SUBSCRIPTIONS
$1.00 per year EACH

CROCKERY AND GLASS JOURNAL
1170 Broadway New York, N. Y.

NEWSNOTES . . . .

T. G. Hawkes & Co.
Redecorates Showroom

Announcement comes from T. G. Hawkes & Co., of Corning, N. Y., that they have enlarged, and have entirely redecorated and re-equipped their New York City showroom at 542 Fifth Avenue; and have announced, also, the completion of their spring lines which are on exhibit there. Penrose Hawkes is in charge of this office.

Coast Firm Lists Prices
Under Fair Trade Act

D. E. Sanford Company, of Los Angeles, San Francisco, and Seattle, according to a recent announcement, has listed all their products and prices with the proper authorities under the California Fair Trade Act. It is believed that the listing of products and prices under the stipulations of the Fair Trade Act in California will do much to destroy the cut price evil. D. E. Sanford is one of the largest coast dealers in china, glass and housewares.

The H. L. Kellys
Vacation in Biloxi

Mr. and Mrs. H. L. Kelly recen ly left Chicago to spend a vacation in the South. They are making their headquarters in Biloxi. Mr. Kelly is a member of the firm of Kelly & Reasner, 1586 Merchandise Mart, Chicago.

Craft Students
League Exhibits

The Craft Students League, a unit of the Y.W.C.A. of the City of New York, held a public exhibit of the work of the students in various crafts from March 18 to 27, in the Squibb Art Galleries at 745 Fifth Avenue, New York. Included in the exhibit were a great many pottery pieces, and included also were exhibits of silversmithing, wood carving, sculpture, weaving, etc. The exhibit was open daily from eleven in the morning until six in the evening. Mrs. Thomas J. Goddard is chairman of the Craft Students League committee of the Y.W.C.A.

Erratum

Announcement was made in last month's news columns of the appointment of sales agents by the Beaver Valley Glass Company in Rochester, Pa. In this item the name of Thomas Jowns, Jr., who will cover the Northwest, and Cleveland, and Detroit for this company, was omitted. There was another error in listing Ernest B. Down as the New England representative, when, in fact, the gentleman's name is E. G. Dower.

THE ITEM FOR THE HOME BAR AND PLAYROOM

Inexpensive and practical because these tumblers can be pushed over or knocked over on the bar or table without breaking or chipping.

In fact owing to greater thickness of glass at bulge—the point of contact—it is practically impossible to break.

PACKED 3 OR 6 DOZ. TO CARTON

CENTRAL GLASS WORKS
WHEELING, W. VA.

#1661—10 oz. SHAM PILSNER BEER
U. S. Design Patent No. 99508

Made in Capacities 1 oz. to 14 oz.

Also in Stem Pilsners

For Hotel Bars or Taverns—Drawn from the Tap One Fill Beer Tumblers.

The bartender makes one draw from the faucet and that is all. Owing to the wider capacity near the top permitting the foam to spread without overflowing the edge.

AGENTS

Francis H. Ruhe, Inc.
14 West 23 St.
N. Y. C.

J. A. Hutchinson
58 E. Wash. St.
Chicago, Ill.

CROCKERY AND GLASS JOURNAL for April, 1937 43

Trade journal ad, pilsner glass, April 1937.

we're all dressed up—
and ready to welcome you in

ROOM 627
NEW YORK HOUSEWARES SHOW
HOTEL PENNSYLVANIA JULY 11-17

Our Latest Creation "*MONTCLAIRE*" Styled Right—Made Right—Priced Right. Many New Decal Patterns and Line Treatments.

STEWART THOMPSON—SALES MANAGER

REPRESENTATIVES

EAST
WILLIAM W. JONES
116 E. Argyle St.
Valley Stream, L. I.
Newland, Schneeloch & Piek
1107 Broadway, New York

MIDWEST
OTTO V. UEBERROTH
Room 15-116, Merchandise Mart
Chicago, Ill.

WEST COAST
A. R. KUHN
4417 Maycrest Ave.
Los Angeles, Calif.
F. W. SANDERS
608 Walnut St.
Little Rock, Ark.

The C.C. THOMPSON POTTERY CO
EAST LIVERPOOL, OHIO

PROTECTED EDGE COCKTAILS

CENTRAL GLASS WORKS
WHEELING WEST VIRGINIA

JUST A FEW OF OUR PRACTICAL ITEMS.

VISIT OUR SHOWROOMS TO SEE COMPLETE LINES

PERMANENT DISPLAY ROOMS

*Francis H. Ruhe, Inc.*
14 W. 23rd St., N. Y. C.

*Jas. A. Hutchinson*
58 E. Washington St., Chi., Ill.

*Himmelstern Bros.*
712 Mission St., San Francisco, Cal.

OR COMMUNICATE WITH THESE SALESMEN

*L. A. Bennett*
293 Beacon St., Boston, Mass.

*Wm. C. Byrnes*
802 Samson St., Philadelphia, Pa.

*Morris Lando*
3708 Central Ave., Cleveland, O.

CROCKERY AND GLASS JOURNAL for July, 1937

Trade journal ad, various cocktail glasses, July 1937.

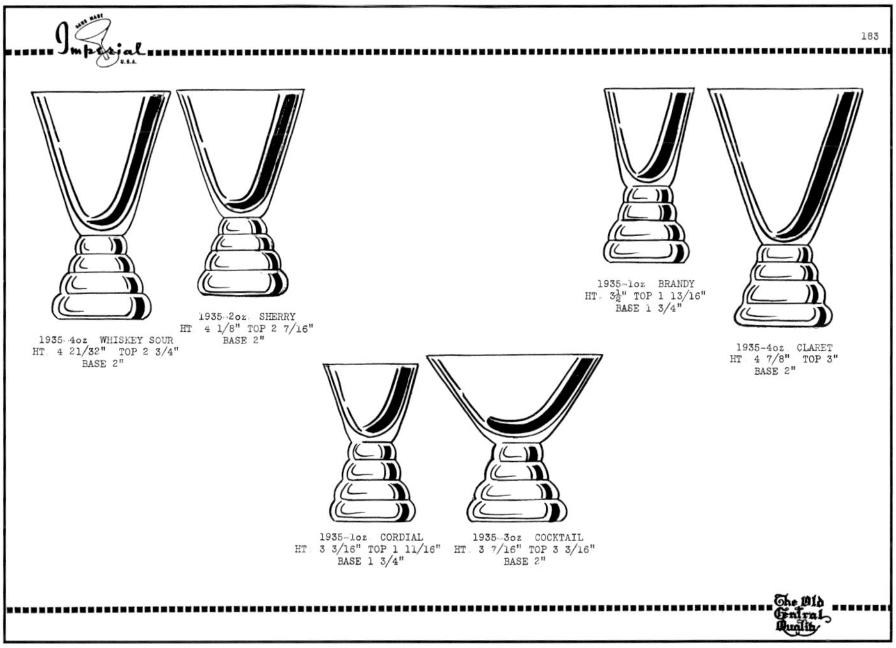


Catalog copy, 1935 line. *Author's catalog.*

Catalog copy, 1937 line. *Author's catalog.*

Catalog copy, 1937 line. *Author's catalog.*

Catalog copy, 1937 line. *Author's catalog.*

Catalog copy, 1938 line. *Author's catalog.*

Catalog copy, 1938 line. *Author's catalog.*

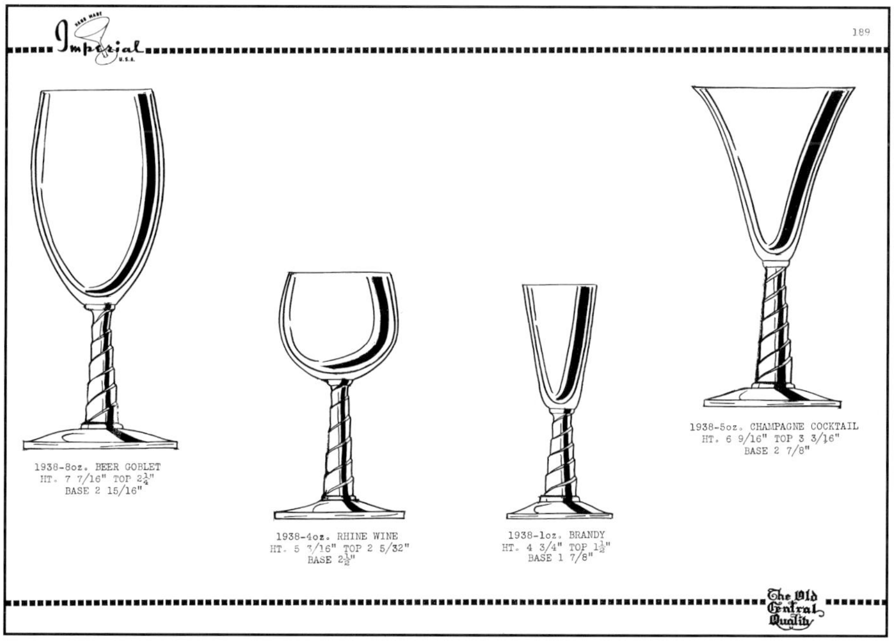


Catalog copy, 1938 line. *Author's catalog.*

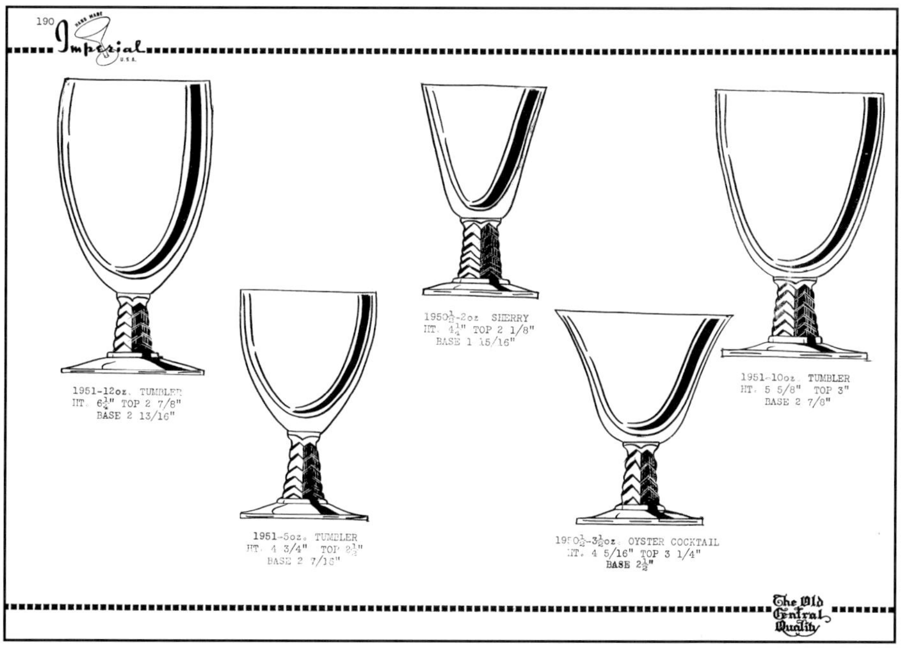


Catalog copy, 1951 line. *Author's catalog.*

Catalog copy, 1951 line. *Author's catalog.*

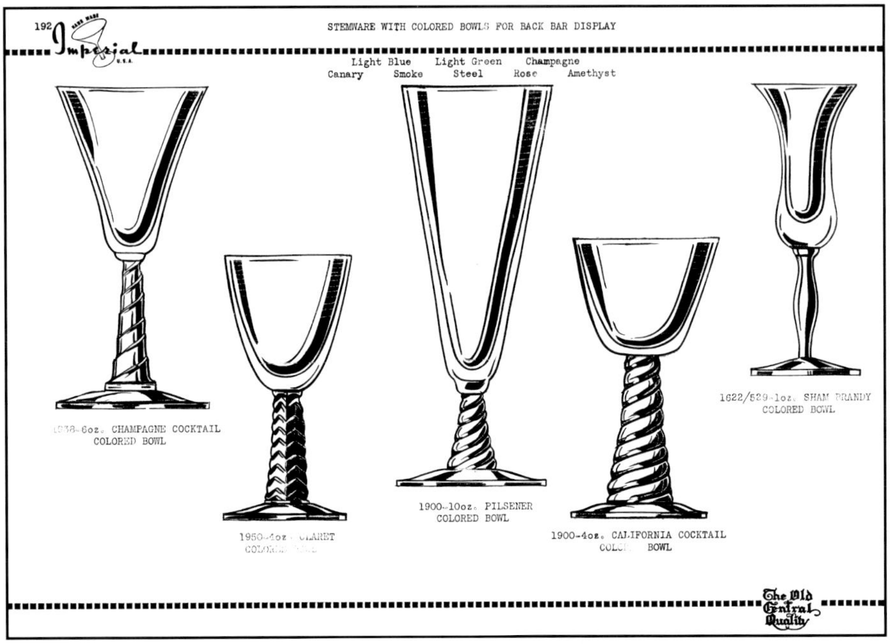


Catalog copy, assorted lines showing colored bowls, where they had been clear bowls with colored stems *Author's catalog.*

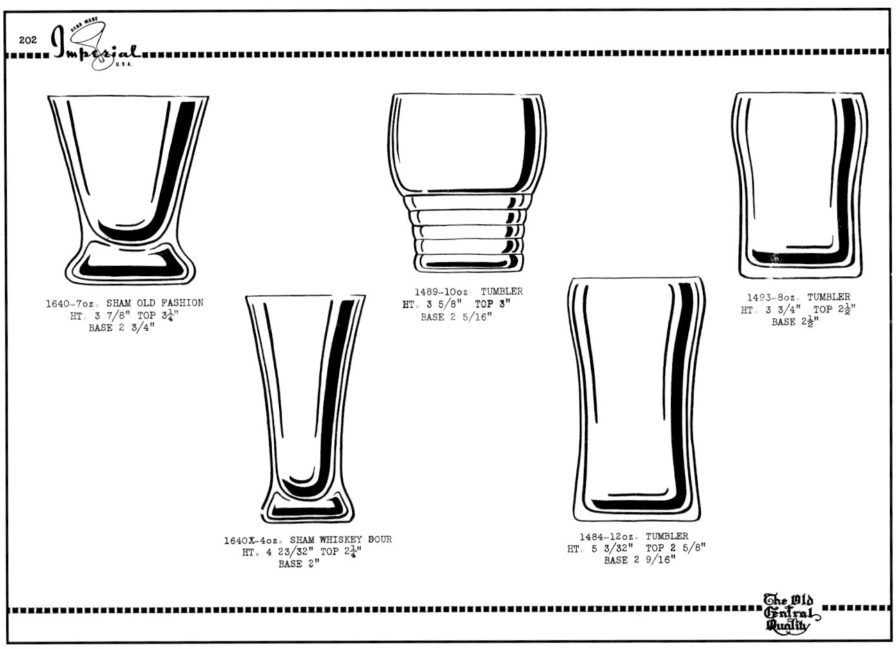


Catalog copy of ribbed tumbler #1489. *Author's Catalog.*

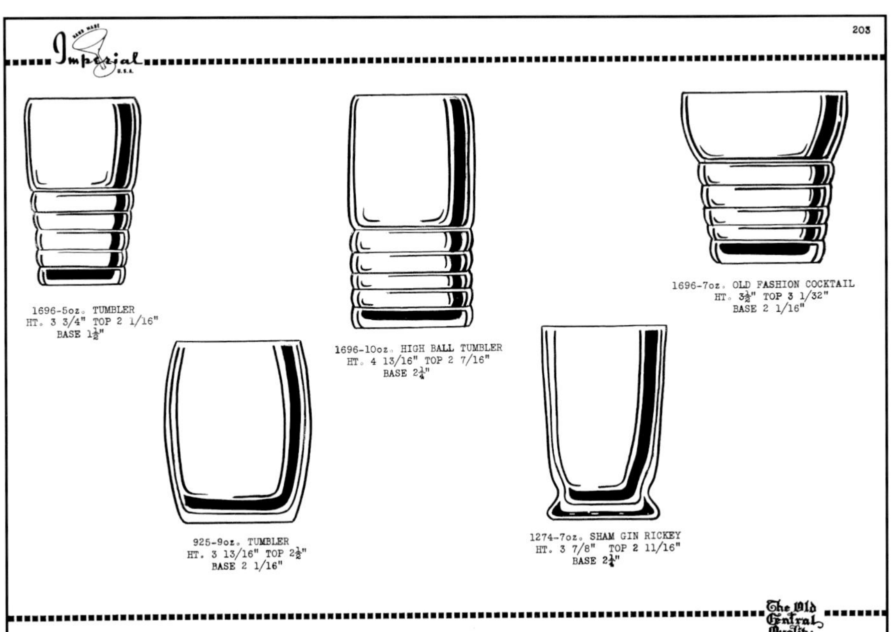


Catalog copy of ribbed tumbler #1696. *Author's Catalog.*

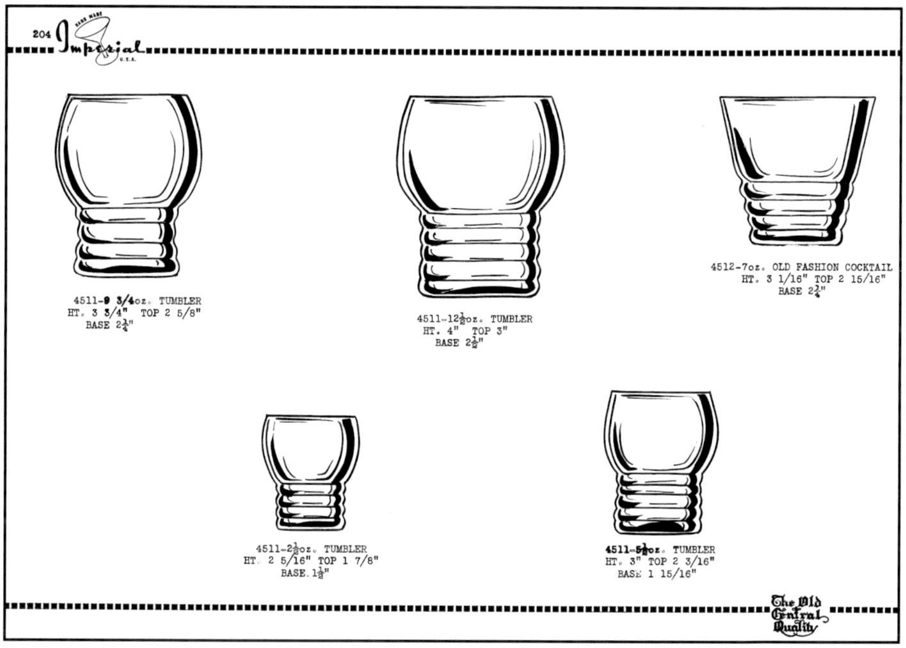


Catalog copy of ribbed tumblers #4511 & 4512. *Author's Catalog.*

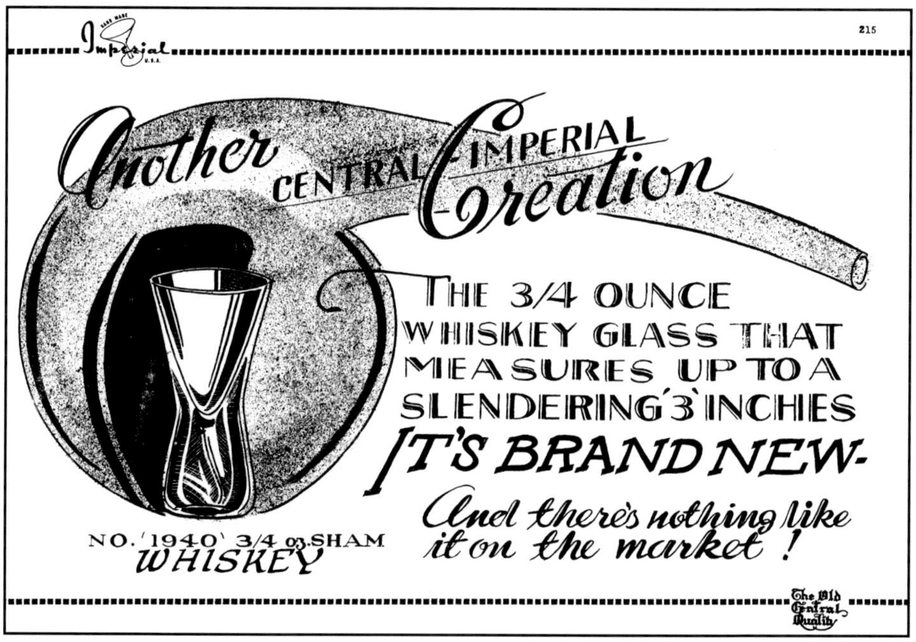


Catalog copy, #1940 Sham. *Author's Catalog.*

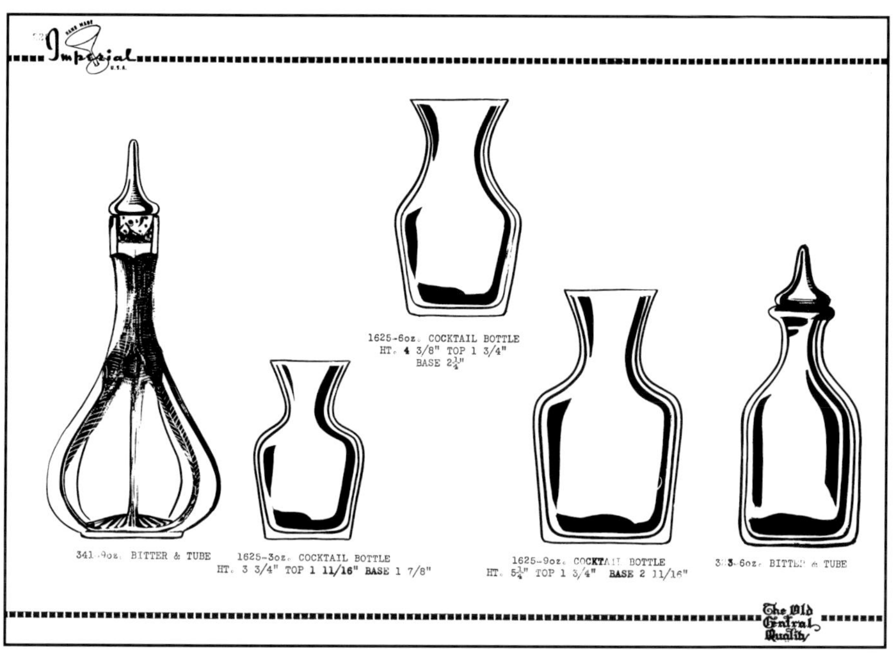


Catalog copy, bar bottles. *Author's Catalog.*

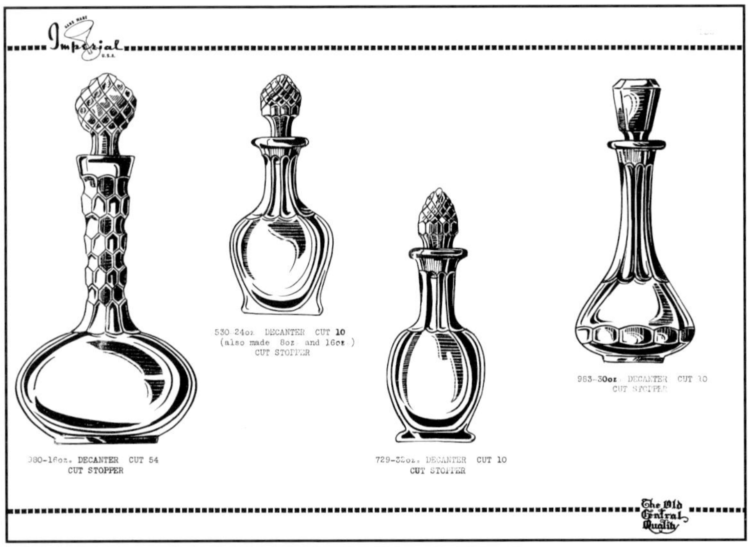


Catalog copy, decanters. *Author's Catalog.*

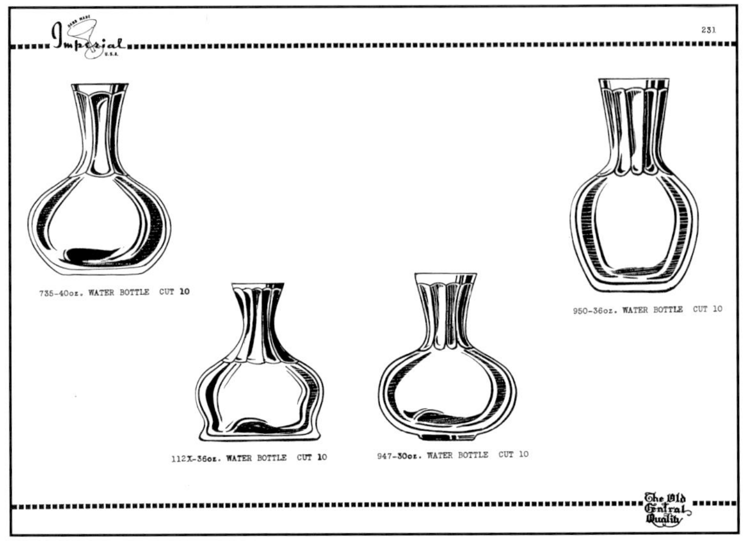


Catalog copy, water bottles. *Author's Catalog.*

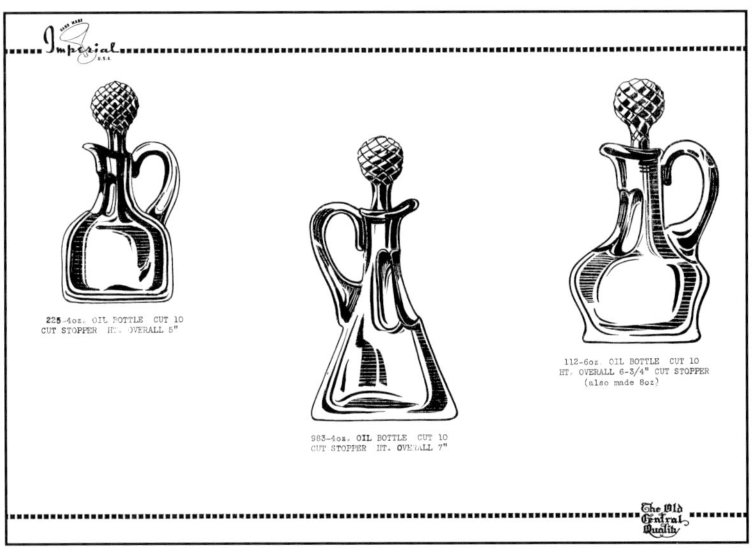


Catalog copy, cruets or oil bottles. *Author's Catalog.*

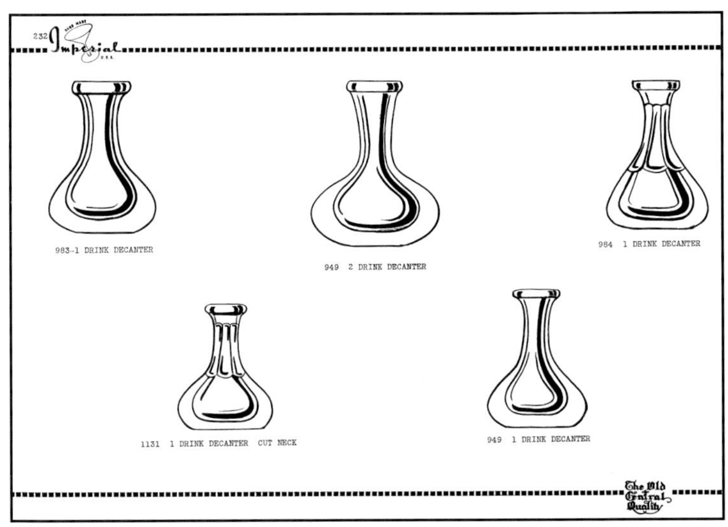


Catalog copy, drink decanters. *Author's Catalog.*

# Other Companies Named Central Glass

During the depression era there were other companies named Central Glass: Central Glass of Summitville, Indiana; Central Glass of Huntington, West Virginia; Louisville, Kentucky; Evansville, Indiana; Chattanooga, Tennessee; Kansas City, Missouri; Central Cut Glass; and Central Glass Company of Urbana, Ohio.

Still even today people are buying what they believe to be rare Central Glass Works art glass items that are actually recently produced pieces from a Central Glass Company in Norman or Spiro, Oklahoma. They write letters and include pictures of their rare piece and show that it still has the sticker attached. The Central Glass Works items that are shown in this reference, and of our collecting interest, were only produced in Wheeling, West Virginia.

Calendar from Central Glass Company, Hutchinson, Kansas.

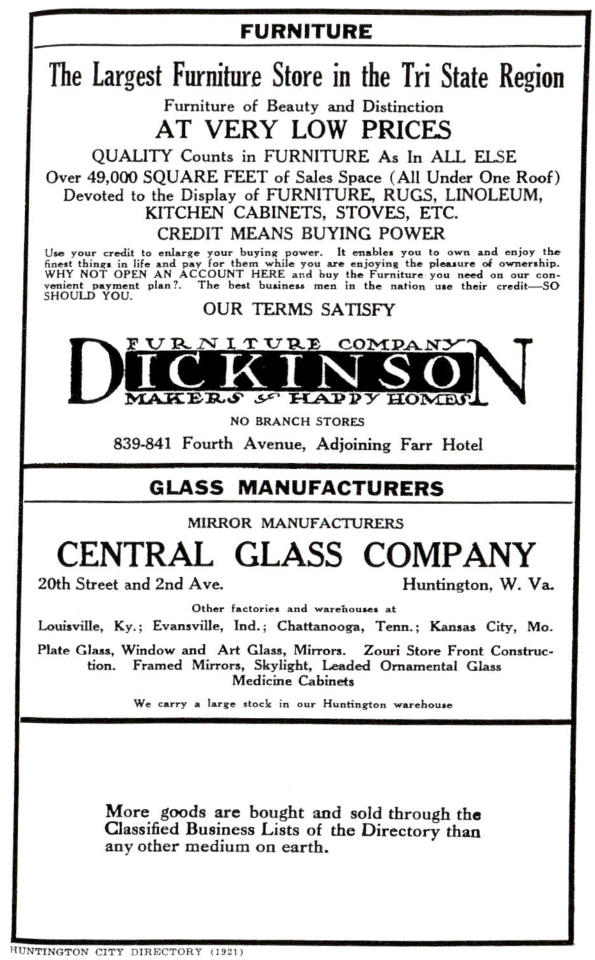

FURNITURE

The Largest Furniture Store in the Tri State Region

Furniture of Beauty and Distinction

AT VERY LOW PRICES

QUALITY Counts in FURNITURE As In ALL ELSE

Over 49,000 SQUARE FEET of Sales Space (All Under One Roof) Devoted to the Display of FURNITURE, RUGS, LINOLEUM, KITCHEN CABINETS, STOVES, ETC.

CREDIT MEANS BUYING POWER

Use your credit to enlarge your buying power. It enables you to own and enjoy the finest things in life and pay for them while you are enjoying the pleasure of ownership. WHY NOT OPEN AN ACCOUNT HERE and buy the Furniture you need on our convenient payment plan?. The best business men in the nation use their credit—SO SHOULD YOU.

OUR TERMS SATISFY

DICKINSON FURNITURE COMPANY MAKERS OF HAPPY HOMES

NO BRANCH STORES

839-841 Fourth Avenue, Adjoining Farr Hotel

GLASS MANUFACTURERS

MIRROR MANUFACTURERS

CENTRAL GLASS COMPANY

20th Street and 2nd Ave. Huntington, W. Va.

Other factories and warehouses at

Louisville, Ky.; Evansville, Ind.; Chattanooga, Tenn.; Kansas City, Mo.

Plate Glass, Window and Art Glass, Mirrors. Zouri Store Front Construction. Framed Mirrors, Skylight, Leaded Ornamental Glass Medicine Cabinets

We carry a large stock in our Huntington warehouse

More goods are bought and sold through the Classified Business Lists of the Directory than any other medium on earth.

HUNTINGTON CITY DIRECTORY (1921)

Ad from Central Glass Company of Huntington, West Virginia, 1921.

# The Glass Company Combines

The first Combine or takeover started in the late 1880s when the United States Glass Company, in an attempt to get better control of the glass market, would attempt to takeover or control over all of the glass producing houses. They did manage to take control of most of the companies, including the Central Glass Company, only to close their doors shortly thereafter. The idea behind such control over all the companies was to give the giant US Glass a larger voice in controlling labor and a bigger voice in lobbying Congress to control tariffs on foreign glassware, which were very low and forcing American Glass producers into hardship.

After Central Glass Works reemerged as a new company in the old building, the National Glass Company was starting a new combine attempt. Around 1899 the National was pushing hard to acquire the Central Glass Works plant of Wheeling, West Virginia. The National had already purchased most of the companies in the region, but Central Glass and the residents of Wheeling were skeptical after their experience with the US Glass takeovers that left many Wheeling residents unemployed. Central Glass fought the National takeover very hard, not wanting to go through another plant shutdown.

Central Glass Works, under the direction of Nathan Bay Scott as President, did manage to fight off the National combine's attempt with the help of the Wheeling business district and citizens, only to watch the Combine fall apart, unable to fulfill their agreements to purchase the glass houses. Many trade journal articles over the following months closing out the century and into the early 1900s discussed the failing of the National Glass Company to produce the cash agreed upon to close the deals with the glass houses. With these failures, most companies returned to their own control, but not before some had fallen to the poorly organized combine attempt.

The Rochester Tumbler Company, a Fry holding, would slip into new business as the Rochester Tumbler Works. The Rochester Tumbler Company had been primarily a jelly jar and pressed tumbler producer, but during the middle of July 1899, during the height of the combine attempt, they had retooled their lines to incorporate new lines of stemware with, in their words, many exciting new lines of blown wares.

The combines did little good for Central Glass Works, with the exception of whatever or however they managed to acquire some of the Rochester Tumbler lines. The National Glass Company did manage one other fantastic feat, the creation of the Cambridge Glass Company in the early 1900s.